PREPARED
for a PURPOSE

Embrace the Process

I0178600

PREPARED
for a PURPOSE
Embrace the Process

Leslie M. Hardy, LCSW, LCAS

Foreword
by Tonya Joyner-Scott

Prepared for a Purpose – Embrace the Process
Copyright © 2018 by Leslie M. Hardy

All rights reserved. No part of this book may be reproduced, stored in a retrieval system, or transmitted in any form or by any means – electronic, mechanical, photocopy, recording, scanning, or other without the prior written permission from the Author.

While the Publisher, Editor and Author have used best efforts in preparing this book to provide accurate and authoritative information in regard to the subject matter covered, no warranties with respect to completeness of the contents are made. This book is not intended to provide nor are the Publisher, Editor and Author engaged in rendering professional or personalized advice or services to the individual reader. This book is sold with the understanding that if expert assistance or counseling is needed in any area, including legal, health, accounting, financial, investment advice, mental or behavioral health, the services of a professional should be sought. The ideas, suggestions and activities contained in this book are not intended as a substitute for such services.

The Publisher, Editor and Author shall not be liable or responsible for any loss or damage allegedly arising from any information or suggestion in this book. The Publisher, Editor and Author specifically disclaim any liability, loss or risk that is incurred as an outcome, directly or indirectly, through the use and application of any contents of this book.

Because of the dynamic nature of the Internet, any web addresses or links contained in this book may have changed since publication and may no longer be valid.

Scriptures marked The Message (MSG) are taken from *The Message*. Copyright © 1993, 1994, 1995, 1996, 2000, 2001, 2002. Used by permission of NavPress Publishing Group.

Scriptures marked NIV are taken from THE HOLY BIBLE, NEW INTERNATIONAL VERSION®, NIV® Copyright © 1973, 1978, 1984, 2011 by Biblica, Inc.® Used by permission. All rights reserved worldwide.

Scriptures marked NKJV are taken from the New King James Version®. Copyright © 1982 by Thomas Nelson. Used by permission. All rights reserved.

Scriptures marked KJV are taken from the New King James Version®. Copyright ©
1982 by Thomas Nelson. Used by permission. All rights reserved.

ISBN-13: 978-0-692-04683-8

Printed in the United States of America

For more information, please contact:
Ms. Leslie M. Hardy
Email: ContactUs@LeslieMHardy.com
Book website: www.p4ap-etp.com

Interior Design: J. Alexander Online
Cover by: Tailiah Breon
Photo Credit: Tailiah Breon / Fashion Prodigy

Dedication

To my Heavenly Father – who has entrusted me with a life of purpose that has brought forth a message of hope, healing, restoration and freedom... not only for me, but for many yet to come. I continue to embrace my process; I trust Him to the expected end!

To my son, Phillip Hardy, who is a gift from God whom "I love to life!" With and through him I have been blessed to know love without limits. He is a constant source of inspiration and encouragement that helps me relentlessly press to become the woman God created me to be, and live in my true purpose.

Acknowledgements

To my family and friends, who have shown unfailing love, gracious support, and continual prayer, and has extended various resources.

To a host of professionals, a few I am honored to know as friends who have influenced my work as we continue to serve others.

To a dear friend who assisted with editorial contributions. I am forever grateful and blessed.

And to anyone who has felt rejected, unloved, or the gnawing ache of loneliness; who has struggled to realize the significance of your life... be encouraged! God has not forgotten you! As you continue your walk of faith and embrace your process, trust that He will fulfill His promises in your life.

Foreword

Often in life we miss the beauty of the process because we devalue the pain. That doesn't make a whole lot of sense to most, does it? To value pain? However, as this book unfolds, you will see that it makes more sense than the average person realizes. I can remember living my life addicted to pain while opposed to valuing it. I constantly lived with an expectation to fail or mess up. Living with a fear of failure and a fear of success made my purpose extremely blurry to me and brought me to a place of standstill with a whole lot of excuses!

The thief of our destiny uses our life experiences in an attempt to destroy us. What you've seen, touched, heard, tasted and smelled goes straight into your memory bank. What people have spoken to you, how it was said, how they looked at you when they said what they said or did what they did registers in your mind. Even what you have smelled during different moments in your life takes up residence in your mind and attaches itself to that moment. Is it a good memory? Is it a memory you wish you didn't have?

The pages in this book take us on a journey of evaluation and discovery. The examples throughout will bring you to a place of reflection and present meditation, propelling you toward your purpose and your future.

Pain's value is simply the ability to identify life's lessons which teach us our strengths and purpose. Its value brings so many descriptions of who we truly are that we may not have otherwise discovered, such as being one who bears the character of God by being powerful, wise, forgiving, loving, patient, kind, and creative just to name a few.

We come to a place of seeing life for the beautiful gift it is, and we look for the purpose in every relationship, interaction, disappointment, hurt, you fill in the blank_____. Leslie's life and her work are shining examples of the powerful verse in the Holy Bible that taught her that *all things would work together for her good, because she loves God and is called according to His purpose* (Romans 8:28).

Prepare to be an overcomer in life by the examples on the following pages.

Tonya Joyner-Scott
The UPgraders

Table of Contents

PREP**A**RED
for a **PURPOSE**
Embrace the Process

Dedication (6)
Acknowledgements (7)
Foreword (8)

Introduction 12

Chapter 1: **Purpose and Process**................................ 15

Chapter 2: **Elements of Process** 31

Chapter 3: **MESSY BeBes**.. 35

Chapter 4: **Choices** 58

Chapter 5: **Influences** 70

Chapter 6: **Thoughts and Beliefs** 83

Chapter 7: **Power of the Mind**................................... 99

Chapter 8: **Change Your Mind, Change Your Life**....................115

Chapter 9: **Now What** 133

Prepared for a Purpose – Embrace the Process 138

Concluding Thoughts...140

Notes...143

Introduction

A vast majority of people have contemplated that relentless inward tug which just seems to not let go and continues to unction us to seek more. It is that tug that sends us searching for what we may unconsciously seek, beyond what we experience through our natural senses of sight, touch, smell, sound, and taste. We long for the truth that keeps us searching for what our hearts deeply yearn. A yearning that goes beyond a powerful career, wealthy bank account, beautiful family, contact list full of friends, and the like. It's this knowing that there has to be more, it's a longing to be filled – it is Purpose!

I was in conversation with a good friend and we were discussing when we respectively discovered our true purpose in life. We both agreed it was when we were in our 40's–she at about 43 and closer to age 48 for me. We are college-educated, mature, responsible women who are mothers, business owners, and personal development professionals. She is also a wife and we both aim to live life intentionally. So, we pondered together how we could be so "accomplished" and just now, in our latter years, embarking on the ultimate fulfillment of life. We knew if we were just getting to this place of realizing and walking in our respective purposes, chances are the next person and likely anyone reading this may be in a similar place.

After reflecting on the matter I concluded that somewhere along the journey of life we encounter detours, distractions, and disappointments which result in decisions made that are inconsistent with our true destiny and delay our walking into our respective purpose. Given the premise that everyone is created for purpose, this book is not about helping you discover or identify your purpose. This book is written to explore the aspect of purpose called *process*, which we all experience as a reality of life.

The *process*, as I identify it, is that which is experienced as a never-ending series of events. Our earlier childhood experiences, thoughts, developing beliefs, mindset, and correlating choices result in what we live as our lives – our present-day realities. This was and has been *the process* of life for my friend and I...and it is *the process* of life for you as well. It is the *process* itself that navigates us through the terrains along our journey to discover our purpose and propels us forward toward it. It is a life course that is unavoidable. And because it is unavoidable, it would probably be helpful to us if we take time to understand what *process* is so we can change how we experience *the process* as it occurs in our lives.

This book is written to explore elements of the *process* of life. It will provide relevant information to help you gain understanding as to why you may be hindered in achieving your goals. It is intended to prepare you to better evaluate your current state, help determine if and what new changes need to be established, and encourage and equip you to make behavioral choices and changes that are consistent with your reaching your destination – your fulfillment of purpose. It is written to help offer you insight and enhance your ability to trust and embrace the inevitable process of life's journey as you begin to see the purpose and value in it.

Chapter 1

Purpose and Process

"Every experience in life has a purpose, though not always readily known. Sometimes the purpose is revealed along the process, as we reflect from the place from which we've grown".

~ Leslie

Right from the start I want to do two things: Introduce you and Invite you. The outcome of your experience with this book hinges on this so - take a deep breath...in deep, out slowly. Once more if needed. Now, let me introduce you to a definitive sense of being that you may have felt within you for a very long time, even if you couldn't find the words to express it.

*S*uccess – to realize and walk in my purpose; to live life fulfilled.

Meditate on that and take another slow, deep, cleansing breath.

Now, if you're ready for the invitation? I invite you to receive the above definition as not only fact but truth. As you allow your thinking to elevate above a limiting definition that's based on what you have or what you do, as you ascend to the beaconing call of what will truly satisfy, know that you are on a journey (your *process)* to your core, your joy...your Purpose!

I'd like to start by sharing with you a bit of my story. I was in my second year of college when I found myself needing money to pay tuition, meals, and room and board for school. To say this was an unexpected situation would be an understatement and I was as equally unprepared. I had not been forewarned my parents would be discontinuing financial support and was therefore caught unprepared with its abrupt end. Though our recollection differs as to why they ceased their financial aid, we all agreed my first semester 1.3 GPA (grade point average) and academic probation had been unacceptable. Ouch!

I could count on two hands how many dates I'd had in high school so it wasn't a far stretch that the new-found freedoms of college proved a bit much for this then shy, sheltered, semi-country girl. My academic performance and financial need were a rude awakening and pivotal point as I began to emerge in that season. Having always been a strong student and my grades being important to me, I recovered and finished my freshman year in good academic standing. To have done otherwise was not really an option. Coming out of high school I had been one of the fortunate few chosen to participate in the InRoads program, largely due to my academics, and I was not about to forfeit that opportunity.

In my opinion, my parents' lack of financial support midway my sophomore year of college really wasn't about my grades at all. Rather, it was the result of

my decision to speak up for myself, in opposition of my father's expectations.
You see, any individual's opinion or will exerted contrary to that of his would
result in immediate backlash – backlash I had repeatedly withstood. That time,
first semester of my sophomore year, my decision to stand my ground would
unknowingly become a clash of wills. It had become an unwelcomed meeting
between me and my father; a meeting long overdue from being necessary to
adjourn.

There is an old English-language proverb, though it is often ascribed to ancient
Greek philosopher Plato that says, "Necessity is the mother of invention,"[1]
meaning "a need or problem encourages creative efforts to meet the need or
solve the problem". Without the financial backing of my parents and not
wanting to take out a loan to continue in school, I was at a crossroads. There I
was. More uncertainty and adversity had introduced themselves in that season,
and being just shy of twenty years of age I felt ill equipped to handle them.
Feeling overwhelmed and scared, I recognized that a 'set time' had presented
itself and I had to make a decision. I could choose to step up or I could settle
and shrink down. **Whether out of fear, foolishness, fortitude, or faith I
decided to step up. I stepped up into the unknown and I willed myself to
move forward** – being certain of this one thing: "Though I may fail my way
into adulthood, I would not remain stagnant in a desolate place." That step of
faith became a step closer to an unknown destiny yet to uncover.

Every individual is given everything he or she needs to be successful in life.
That means that each of us is born with unlimited possibility, heartfelt desires,
and an untamed imagination. As little children, we, innocently and without
inhibition, express the things that we want, with all the imagination and faith we

can muster. We believe the world is ours to explore and enjoy. We are wide-eyed, optimistic, daring and unstoppable! We believe we can do anything and everything we want to do! Remember such a time in your life? What about a time when someone reminded you of how you were a daring and imaginative child?

*D*o you remember those earlier years when someone who believed in you asked what you wanted to be when you grew up? Likely you enthusiastically and unapologetically resounded, "I want to be...!" or "I want to do....!". There was no hesitation in your response. You didn't stop and ponder how you would do it or if you could become it, whatever the 'it' was. You didn't consider any of the 'what ifs' because they had no place in your mind of possibilities. All you believed was that you wanted what you wanted, and so it would be! You would have it no matter what!

Does any of that sound remotely familiar? Can you feel the excitement now, in this moment thinking about it, as you did then?

The purity and possibilities of our childlike faith likely dissipated as we grew older and were inevitably impacted and shaped by **life**. Life! The series of events, experiences, interactions, reactions and opportunities that make up our journey through this world. Life! The journey that culminates and resets daily as it intersects with the many different people we encounter. Life! The gift we've been given to discover, open, enjoy and share as we take ownership of our own.

"Life is never made unbearable by circumstances,
but only by lack of meaning and purpose."
~Viktor Frankl[2]

Little had I known my sophomore year in college that I was embarking on a journey (a phase along my *process*) that would set me in motion to fulfill my purpose. That season of time began to definitively shape the person I would become. It set me on a path where I would continue to grow stronger, more determined, and faith-filled in perseverance. It led me to a place where I would become an advocate and someone better equipped to face life's challenges. It helped inform and qualify me to inspire and empower others in embracing their inevitable *process* to realize their purpose in life.

"Man's search for meaning is the primary motivation in his life..."
~Viktor Frankl[3]

Our journeys through life are unique with different commonalities along the way. Whether destined to take the long, dusty tobacco roads of eastern North Carolina, the edgy mountain trails of the New Hampshire Franconia Ridge, the banks of the Louisiana Bayou, the "quaint" city streets of Omaha, or the bustling city blocks of New York City, *the process* we experience is both inevitable and the same, although we each travel different terrains. That *process* is what's known as a necessary part of our preparation for purpose.

PROCESS

Webster defines *Process* as "a series of actions or steps taken in order to achieve a particular end." However, *Process* as I refer to it here is never-ending. What do I mean? As long as we are living, we will always be in a "*process*". We will always be in the state of undergoing change, and change is never stagnant. This means that as we change, we continue to go through *process*. That said, the goal then is to keep going and progress through, **to** our NEXT, our next level of *process*. *Process is the means whereby we journey through life and attain information to become equipped and prepared to be most successful in realizing and walking in our purpose.* We'll explore more about this as you continue to read.

How long we exist in or pass through any given stage of *process* may vary and will depend on different things. But the fact of our actually being in some form of *process* remains the same. So, it's not a matter of *if* we are in the position or plight of *process*; rather, it is *how* we choose to go through the *process*. And the better we understand it, the more we can choose to *embrace the process;* allowing it to further develop, mature, and change us for the better.

"Change is not an event, it's a process."
~ Cheryl James[4]

The life changing circumstances I faced my sophomore year in college were just a few that would prove to challenge and thus change me. With the money I had saved from my InRoads internship and a $500 loan from a family member, I was able to finish out my sophomore year. With no idea how I would pay to stay in school, I became aware of an opportunity to earn an unlimited amount of money during the summer, which seemed like a good idea.

Young, naïve, and excited about traveling out of state with the potential to earn an unlimited amount of money, I set out on my first entrepreneurial endeavor on 'the book field.' The book field was a commission based, direct sales opportunity with the possibility to earn a free trip to the Bahamas! I was in need of money, not just for school but for my on-going daily living expenses; so applying Plato's philosophy, my venture in direct sales was that 'creative effort' I engaged to meet a definite need.

I would soon find out that working on the book field would not be a typical summer job. Setting out on my inaugural book field undertaking, a group of us caravanned from North Carolina to Tennessee for a week-long training at the corporate offices. Though we had received local based training during the school year to prepare for our summer work, we gained invaluable training at the corporate office in the principles of sales and personal development by some of the best, including legendary great, Zig Ziglar and Mort Utley!

At the end of a week of training we all dispersed to our respective territories, with me heading to Memphis, Tennessee. I travelled to another state where I knew no one, would work for a non-guaranteed wage, and had to locate and secure my own safe, affordable lodging. I'm sure to some this seemed crazy. Maybe. To me, it was necessary. My objective was to make enough sales (by sharing the product information and its benefits in such a way that the prospective buyer could see its value and choose to purchase) to finance my way through each of the remaining years of college. And following the training, atmosphere, and expectations that had been set in those few days at corporate, I was very excited and I guess you could say I was *ignorance on fire!* Little did I know what a significant event that would become in my life.

Within a few hours upon arrival in Memphis, I'd found and negotiated summer housing and fees for my roommate and I, each of us having our own room. Though that was a huge hurdle cleared, offering some immediate relief to this new model of work, it would soon pale in comparison to what was to come. The book field definitely afforded me an indelible experience of independence unlike anything I'd ever known.

How we choose to go through our *process* experience is dependent upon what we think about it, our attitude and feelings concerning it, our beliefs, and the related choices we make therein. It is this recipe of our thoughts, attitudes and emotions, beliefs, and choices that will dictate the direction in which we move through life – either progressively or regressively – in relation to our desired plans, passions, and purpose of greatness.

Having started this book field venture with less than $200 to last me a couple of weeks, it was only in hindsight that I realized what a walk of faith this would be. How my life perspective would change. The book field was an undertaking where I readily recognized that it was solely my decision as to whether or not I would:

- get up and go to work on any given day;
- work all day, from 9:00am until usually 7:00pm;

- walk alone, door-to-door knocking on strangers' doors in a place where I knew no one and nothing about the city;

- carry all that was needed, making my work bag 40 lbs heavy, while walking all day;

- work outside, rain or shine in 90+ degree weather;

- surrender to the idea of a guaranteed hourly wage in terms of a typical job and secure one while on location for the summer when funds were low, knowing a job would pay far less than what could be earned on the commissioned based book field;

- pack my lunch or spend funds to eat out;

- work until the goal was met...or rationalize why it was okay to end my day early without the sales I needed;

- continue through the rejection, bad attitudes, and the "nos" received from people who did not even want to hear what I had to offer.

It had become painfully clear that it was my decision just what I would do. It was a time of choices and consequences for which there was no reneging – no turning back. There was no bank account to withdraw from. There was no money coming from my parents and everyone around me was hustling to do the same thing – make money to meet a goal. I knew if I didn't work, there was a grave likelihood I would go without in the present, and worse, not have the money I needed to pay for school the following year. Both served as great motivators to get up and out each morning.

"It is not enough that we do our best;
sometimes we must do what is required."
~ Winston S. Churchill[5]

I started out that summer with a plan to earn the money I needed to cover all of my college expenses and pay back a $500 loan from a family member, and I did. I earned more money that summer than I had collectively earned all my life. I also learned something that money alone would have never been able to offer! Mr. Mort Utley summed up my experience precisely during a keynote speech he gave one summer to the students of our program:

"You're going to have the greatest summer than you've ever had in all of your lives. You're going to earn more money than you ever thought was possible in a 13-week period. But far more important than that money, if you go out on the book field this summer and do the things you've been trained to do in the way you've been trained to do them, **you're going to build within yourselves some qualities that will follow you and help you the rest of your lives. You will develop some habits of life!** *And these qualities and these habits will make you better husbands, better wives*
...... No matter what you do or become in this world, you will be better at it because of the Southwestern experience."
~ Mort Utley[6]

He was right. My moving forward despite the apprehension I had embraced less than 12 weeks prior had resulted in an afresh, bittersweet independence.

My act to capitulate to the fear laid the groundwork for a significant step of faith. Moreover, the step of faith taken out of pure necessity proved to be life changing!

I was able to finance my remaining two years of college working the summer months on the book field in direct sales! Put another way, I invested only 6 months of time to finance two years of college education. That was a wise investment. I did not **have** to work during the fall and spring semesters of the following years while carrying a full academic load. Working was optional, yet I opted to work!

Process is the means whereby we journey

through life and attain information to become

equipped and prepared to be most successful in

realizing and walking in our purpose.

I have found there is a lot to be gained from working other than the financial compensation. When approached with the proper heart, attitude, and mindset to learn as much as possible, work can be transformative. The lack of college financial aid was a great catalyst which exposed me to many 'firsts' that put me in a position to make decisions about things I had not previously faced. Prior to my introduction to the book field, the idea of unlimited income or my determining my income was just an ideal; something I imagined with no plan to see it through. Yet an unwelcomed clash of wills accompanied by unexpected financial need would become the impetuous gateway of an experience that would unlock and propel me to uncommon possibilities – to explore, dream bigger and beyond the obvious limitations that had previously been constructed, unknowingly within my own mind.

The encounter of the book field was a springboard to new milestones of personal development and performance that shifted my focus, self-confidence, and who I was to become. The free cruise trip I earned to the Bahamas was just icing on the cake! My first taste and glimpse of the life I *somehow* knew I wanted to live. It was a defining place along my *process* that was to further develop my character, increase my faith, and direct me toward my purpose and destiny in life, to craft my best life.

"Life shrinks or expands in proportion to one's courage."
~ Anaïs Nin[7]

Though I had certainly weathered challenges my first couple of decades, my book field experience had expanded my mind, my life, my confidence, and my faith to encompass a new dimension of courage – never for me to be the same again. Still, what I didn't know at that time was there were unforeseen hurdles yet for me to bound along my pathway to maturity and growth...to the life I now more consciously imagined. Unbeknownst to me, there were hidden obstructions that had been erected during the earlier stages of my journey – those important, formative years of development in childhood.

Sometimes, and I dare say oftentimes, while venturing through life toward our purpose (the essence of our journey that gives life meaning), we face situations we are ill-equipped to handle, or settle in places we had not intended to remain. This is due in large part to the **"MESSY BeBes"** (Mental, Emotional, Self-Sabotage Yielding Beliefs and Behaviors) we form and adopt along the way.

"MESSY BeBes" *are*

<u>M</u>ental, <u>E</u>motional <u>S</u>elf-<u>S</u>abotage <u>Y</u>ielding

<u>B</u>eliefs and <u>B</u>ehaviors *that we*

unknowingly, subconsciously develop and

adopt during our process.

Many of us have come through places during our *process* where we faced challenges, tackled obstacles, and pushed through adversities and disappointments while trying to hold on to faith and belief. Through my own *process* (including both my personal life and professional experiences in the behavioral mental health field) I have learned how and helped others to effect positive change through the release and *re*purposing of **MESSY BeBes.** That discovery has become my message – a message of inspiration, encouragement, hope, and healing.

In his book, *The 15 Invaluable Laws of Growth*, leadership expert and author John C. Maxwell shares that "to discover your purpose, you need to grow in self-awareness." That's literally what this book is about. Throughout these pages we're going to examine and expose some things to help position you to grow. Based on what I've observed and learned about life's journey, we will delve into how and why it's necessary for you to **embrace the life-long *process* that prepares us for our purpose.** We will explore the magnitude of the mind, the power of personal choice, and the importance of faith.

I'm here to encourage you. No matter where you find yourself today, it is possible to change the course of your life, achieve desired goals, and realize your purpose...as you embrace your *process*!

"What we are waiting for is not as important as what happens to us while we are waiting. Trust the process."

~ Mandy Hale[8]

Chapter 2

Elements of *the Process*

"You must take personal responsibility.
You cannot change the circumstances,
the seasons, or the wind, but you can change yourself.
That is something you have charge of."
~ Jim Rohn [1]

We all have been created on purpose for a purpose. That is established from the beginning and does not change. How we reach our purpose has everything to do with our *process*. *Process* is a never-ending journey that, while constant in its persistence, varies in its presentation. The maturation of our *process* requires time, effort, patience.

I define three main elements to *process*. These three elements are the foundation to understanding our *process*, how we respond in life, which in turn helps us to identify why we do what we do and what to focus on in order to create different results in our life. These three elements are:

1. Action - what we experience in life,

2. Belief - what we believe to be true about that we experience,

3. Choices - what we choose to do (or the consequence) as a result of what we believe about the experience.

Action (What we experience in life) are those events that occur in our life as a result of our own actions, the actions of others, or those actions seemingly beyond our control. This can include things such as a new job or school, divorce, a pat on the back, or a medical condition. Outside of the stimuli we process through our 5 senses, actions in and of themselves are not necessarily positive or negative, they are relatively neutral. They take on a positive or negative connotation based on how we experience the actions or what we believe about the actions. The way we experience actions is based on our filters – filters developed over time by previous experiences. An example of action is *being encouraged to try your best, as a child, and being praised for your efforts.*

Belief (What we trust to be true about what we experience) speaks to our awareness of our thoughts, emotions, and our beliefs. From the beginning of our existence, we are being bombarded with information that passes through our senses – taste, sight, smell, touch, sound – that in turns gets recorded and stored in our memory banks. As we grow and experience life, we begin to adopt certain thoughts or perceptions about the information or experiences that we have had as "truth". These truths become imbedded in our mind as part of our belief system and impacts how we perceive life and continue to go forth in our experience of the world. Building on the above example, *if you experience being encouraged to try your best and are praised for your efforts as a child, you likely grow to believe you are capable, valued, and loved.*

Choices (What we decide to do as a result of what we believe) is the way we decide to respond to any given experience based on what we believe to be true about what it is we have experienced. Many people think because we *say* we believe something then *it is so* and *true* for us. If that were the case, then we all could say we are _____ (fill in the blank) and it would happen or be for us. But we all know life just doesn't happen that way. The reason is because in our heart of hearts, we don't actually *believe* everything we say and think on and therefore we are not moved to act upon it. The simple truth is we act based on what *we believe to be true*, not necessarily what we say or think is true or even what actually is true. The key here is, if you believe "it" is true, (whatever "it" is for you) whether it actually is true or not, "it" will be true **to** you! Continuing further with our example, *if you are encouraged to try your best and are praised for your efforts as a child, you likely grow to believe you are capable, valued, and loved; therefore, you likely will try new things, develop self-confidence, and have a more balanced outlook on life.*

The above overviews give you an idea of how the three elements work together to form the foundation for how we experience life. They are the foundation upon which we continue to build and plan our lives and are key to how we go about fulfilling our life's purpose. I will expound on the elements more in later chapters. Hopefully though you can see and readily understand that it is important we develop a solid, healthy foundation in our *process* or do the work to strengthen an existing poor foundation. This is important because every experience we have informs and impacts the next experience we have, no matter how big or small.

Someone once shared with me an account regarding a newly constructed house that did not pass inspection because there were issues with its foundation! Can you imagine? The builder had not taken the time and care to ensure the foundation was properly laid so that the structure of the home would be adequately supported, thereby ensuring the quality of the house built. This is a good analogy of what happens in our lives from the beginning.

*W*hen care is not taken to ensure we have the proper foundation laid (i.e., nurturance of a positive self-esteem and confidence, proper self-image, capacity to show empathy, compassion, love, understanding, etc. – all which further support our development as healthy individuals and our success in realizing our purpose in life), there is grave potential for the development of cracks, instability, deficits, and what I call **MESSY BeBes**.

For us, our heart or spirit performs the inspection of the foundation in our lives. It lets us know if there is something misaligned that needs correcting, and our behaviors are its evidence. It is up to us to recognize or acknowledge the cracks in our foundation, take steps to repair them, and be repositioned to a place of correction in order to fulfill our purpose.

"People are never able to outperform their self-image."

~ John C. Maxwell [2]

Chapter 3

MESSY BeBes

"No factor is more important in people's psychological development and motivation than the value judgments they make about themselves."
~ Nathaniel Branden[1]

You may be wondering, "What is this **MESSY BeBes**"? I was a bit surprised when this concept just seemingly "downloaded" into my mind one day as I was writing this book. I just smiled as I realized what had just happened as I allowed the idea to evolve. Once it was clear to me how to proceed, the idea was further developed with the help of a friend to what has now been coined **MESSY BeBes**. This process, how **MESSY BeBes** was created, is an example of how "thoughts" can become things and yes, it can happen just like that, in an instant! Too often we can be caught up in the routine cares of life and miss such a divine design, which I believe this was. So, pay attention to your thoughts and recognize their source.

MESSY BeBes, pronounced "messy babies", was established as a play on words to make its meaning easy to remember. It is a light-hearted but purposed acronym which represents the "<u>M</u>ental, <u>E</u>motional <u>S</u>elf-<u>S</u>abotage <u>Y</u>ielding <u>B</u>eliefs and <u>B</u>ehaviors" that we unknowingly, subconsciously develop and adopt during our *process*. Let's start with the BeBes (babies).

When we think of human babies, especially if we have had any of our own, most people think of cute, cuddly, soft little people who are innocent, loveable, and a blessing. They come into our lives and are the source of much love and joy. If you are a parent or desire to be a parent, I'm sure you know what I mean. Most parents are more than willing to do all they can to supply for their baby's every need. And without even a thought, babies do what comes naturally to get their needs met. They coo or babble when they are content. They may whine or cry when they need to be changed, perhaps are in pain, or when they are hungry and need to be fed. Once babies are fed their little bodies' just do what they need to in order to complete the digestion process and eliminate waste...they poop! Oftentimes their poops create a mess that has to be cleaned up. This is symbolic of life's *process* which produces our **MESSY BeBes**. Allow me to share this real, practical visual with you.

I was visiting my cousin shortly after the concept of **MESSY BeBes** was formed when I observed his precious, happy-go-lucky, just-learning-to-walk daughter wobble across the floor. She smiled as she periodically clapped her little hands and bobbled from side to side in her style of dance, making unintelligible yet joyful sounds of conversation without a care in the world.

It didn't seem to matter at all to her that out of her little body projected a secretion accompanied by a foul smelling green liquid seeping out of the top of her diaper, bleeding visibly through her white onesie. While the smell caused the adults in the room to have facial contortions and mutter about the odor, she was seemingly completely unaware of her mess or its lingering effects. This illustration is symbolic of what all too often happens mentally and emotionally in our lives.

"Love can change a person the way a parent can change a baby- awkwardly, and often with a great deal of mess."
~ Lemony Snicket[2]

*T*he way a lot of people were 'loved or treated' as children (which may not have been love at all) can and does create *mess,* which unfortunately results in negative effects that show up unrecognized along the way in beliefs and behaviors. Many of us go through life not aware of the **MESSY BeBes** that have formed until much later in our lives; thus, we are unaware of how those MESSY BeBes have impacted and are impacting others and ourselves.

The mess that was produced from my baby cousin's body did not come from no where or nothing. It started with the green peas she had been fed. As a child she didn't have a choice about what she was fed, she only consumed what she was fed. Once she had eaten what she had been fed it then passed through her digestive system where it was processed to supply her body with nutrients.

After her body was finished processing what she had ingested, her body released the resulting waste. Take note, she didn't eat the peas and then excrete the peas in its original form. *The pea had to go through an unseen, internal process* in order to be useful to her, and *the **process*** wasn't completed until she released the waste. And though we can't see *the process* itself as it's taking place, the poop provides evidence that *the process* has occurred and successfully completed!

From our own experiences, we know that the length of the digestive process can take hours, sometimes days, and even weeks for some, before the residual waste is released. In fact, medically if someone is not eliminating digestive waste in a timely manner it can cause bloating, toxic buildup, and other issues such that there is cause for great concern and the condition has to be addressed.

So it is with our **MESSY BeBes**. Our **MESSY BeBes** are formed from the elements of our life *process* – the things we experience, how we internalize our experiences, and what we choose to do as a result. And as it is with the little ones who create a physical mess in their diapers that we take care to clean up, so it is with our **MESSY BeBes** once *the process* is completed! There are **MESSY BeBes** we must clean up.

There is a principle, 'whatever is in you, is that which will come out of you', literally and figuratively. As stated earlier, many of us go through life not realizing the impact **MESSY BeBes** have on our daily lives and the lives of those around us. Therefore, **MESSY BeBes** (Mental, Emotional, Self-sabotage Yielding Beliefs and Behaviors) can form during and linger after any given phase of *our process*. That's why it is imperative that proper care is taken and observed as we matriculate through the *process* of life and proper cleaning is conducted as needed throughout. Keep in mind the *elements of the process*:

1) what we experience (Action),

2) what we think, feel, and believe about what we experience (Belief),

3) what we do as a result (Choices).

These elements of *process* go through an internal procedure, producing the very things we say, do, and believe that too often are the opposite of what is actually true about us – who we are created to be. These **MESSY BeBes** form very early on and develop over time, having been deposited in our mental bank, drawing interest.

*T*hey become thoughts, habits, and beliefs that grow big, strong, and practically unnoticed for months, years, and decades throughout our lives. They become such an ingrained part of our being that we become oblivious to their existence and subsequent ramifications. People influenced by **MESSY BeBes** can typically be heard saying things at various times such as, "That's just the way I am" or "I can't help it". And at one time or another, that has been all of us!

Chains of habit are too light to be felt until they are too heavy to be broken.
~ Warren Buffet[3]

MESSY BeBes crawl around in our subconscious undetected until they show up and show out in ways reflective of how we actually think and feel, particularly about ourselves – which is typically "less than". Less than... smart enough, pretty enough, tall enough, small enough, good enough, etc.

They are a result of the false, inaccurate, and harmful things, sometimes which may be outright lies that are said or done toward us that we internalize as being true, yet they do not align with our true self. In fact, they may not be true at all, though we receive them as true. **Enough**, of not enough! We must choose and learn how to be done with that!

This concept of **MESSY BeBes** reminds me of a situation which occurred concerning my son, Phillip, when he had just entered kindergarten – a profound moment along his *process* as well as that of my own as a parent. Pay attention as this story takes time to unfold.

I was a single mother a year out of graduate school and excited about my first career job. I had been uncommonly blessed with a position as a child and family psychotherapist which required my traveling a congested and stressful 45 - 60 minutes, one-way commute to and from work–uncommon in that I had no prior experience. That was favor!

When I accepted my job position I also decided to purchase my first home. I knew I needed to shorten my commute so I looked for a property that would be closer and in a great school district. I was fortunate to purchase a home directly across the street from what would be my son's new school. I had purposed to be an intentional parent. Wanting to be as involved as possible, I reasoned the school's proximity would help eliminate certain barriers.

That summer prior was a fun time of Power Rangers, Ninja Turtles, Rugrats, and Looney Tunes. Don't judge me. He didn't know it but I wanted him to enjoy those last days of 'pre'-school as I realized we were entering a new phase of life. Enthusiastically anticipating its start, we had prepared by visiting the school, meeting the administrators and staff, and talking about Phillip's excitement and our expectations. He'd experienced the attendance of daycare which I had routinely referenced with him as 'school' so he looked forward to his rite of passage.

With my commute, it was necessary for Phillip to attend his school's early arrival program, making for long days. Eager and just as nervous for his first day, I drove him to the front of the school, placed the car in park, and transitioned to walk around to the rear passenger door. I had imagined this day for months, looking forward to walking my handsome, bright, energetic little five-year old into school.

There were no teachers to greet the students curbside so I was also expected to walk him in. Just as quick as I could get around the back of the car, Phillip had gotten out and walked 5 yards ahead before turning around and giving me the universal hand signal for 'STOP!'

Quite surprised, I complied with the gesture and stopped right in my tracks to hear him exclaim, "No mommy! You don't have to come with me. I'm not a baby. I can do it (go into the school) by myself!"

"Say what!!! Oh, no he didn't!" were the thoughts that seared across my mind. For a split second my feelings were hurt as I absorbed the veracity of his words. No, he was not a baby...but he would always be my baby.

I stood paralyzed in the sadness of that truth, suppressing the tears that were on the cusp of an overflow.

Though a bit startled by his quick assertion of autonomy, I was still undoubtedly pleased with my son's determination and assuredness. It was his first day of public school and he was passionate to embrace it single handedly.

I on the other hand reluctantly watched, not having moved a step beyond his command. I stood and watched as he joyfully entered the building looking back to give me a quick wave. I smiled as I waved back and declared for him to, "Have a good day!" just before the door closed behind him...seconds shy of my facial waterfall.

My baby was growing up. We had turned the page to the start of another chapter of our lives.

I'm sure I didn't always get it right nor do everything best all the time, but one thing I had definitely been mindful of doing was communicating positive information and affirmation to my son about who he was and what he could do. Being an African-American little boy, I was aware of the challenges he faced in this world just based on that fact alone and I wanted to at least give him a good start by affirming who he was created to be.

Every experience we have informs and

impacts the next experience we have, no

matter how big or small.

It had only been three hours since the start of the *first day* of kindergarten when I received a call from his teacher. She reported my son would not sit still in his seat, was sliding out of his chair, and crawling around under the tables. After a couple of minutes of her expounding about her frustrations, she asked if I had any ideas of how she could curtail Phillip's behavior – a laughable situation now in retrospect but it definitely wasn't then. I wish I could say I was surprised to have gotten the call, but sadly I was not.

A bit disheartened to have received a call so soon, I tried to empathize with the teacher's position as I offered what I considered to be a reasonable rationale explanation for my son's described behavior. The fact that he was in a new school, with a new teacher, in a class of unfamiliar faces (most of which did not have his same complexion) were all plausible reasons I offered to help reframe her perception of his behaviors – none of which seemed too acceptable to her.

I wanted to be helpful as I believed my son's actions were not to be that of blatant disruption but that of a child who was probably exhibiting some anxiety. And so it began – the consistent need for my advocacy to bring a corrective experience for the fair and just treatment for my son.

Remember what I'd shared earlier? It takes more than just *saying* a thing for it to be true. The words alone are not enough. In order for something to be true to an individual, it has to be heard or thought, received or held onto as true, and believed. Once someone believes information as truth, they will begin to act as such and create a reality according to those beliefs. Herein was my concern.

Over the next several weeks of my son's kindergarten experience I was especially mindful of his attitude and behavior regarding school. I became aware through my conversations and interactions with Phillip that he felt he was "getting in trouble" for doing things he had observed other students doing. Those same students were apparently not "getting in trouble" or receiving any type of consequence, at least not that Phillip could observe. He on the other hand was being sent out of the classroom to another teacher's class or to the principal's office on frequent occasions because of his presupposed behavior. He described what he was experiencing as "unfair".

I had noticed his initial upbeat disposition toward school was becoming more solemn and subdued. I knew something was amiss and had made efforts to assist the teacher toward successful solutions. I had arranged with my supervisor to take extended lunch hours to drive to his school, unannounced, to drop in and see what was going on. On more than one occasion I arrived to find my son had been sent out of his class yet again, without my knowledge.

I wanted and was willing to give the teacher reasonable time to work out whatever issue she was having with my son, as I continued to monitor the situation. That was until the one and only day she called, not to engage me in a collaborative dialogue, but to state the fact that 'she didn't know what kind of time I spent with (my) son' and rhetorically questioned if he was even "supervised outside of school." She proceeded to say she didn't "know what to do with him and his behaviors" and she indicated she wanted to "refer him to the school support team to be evaluated".

Being 8-10 weeks into the school year and with my having attempted, albeit unsuccessfully, to work with this teacher to understand and address whatever issues she had concerning my son, it became painfully obvious that she only seemed vested in a resolution that involved a school referral. Now if you've been paying attention, you can probably guess my response.

As parents, it is vitally important we are

involved and aware of our children's school

environment and even more, aware of how

the environment affects them.

In light of all my best efforts and the information I had gathered, I had deduced this teacher was the problematic factor in this equation. It appeared most of the 'problems' she reported were due in essence to her apparent racial bias, beliefs, inequitable classroom treatment and her unwillingness to receive my feedback or make changes in and of herself.

Not only were her actions negatively impacting the students' perceptions of my son in her class but her treatment of him had begun to gravely impact his own self-image! This same child whom had been excited and eager about school just 2 months prior was now reluctant and resistant to even going!

*T*he interactions, behavior, communication, and environment that had been fostered within that classroom were precisely the habitat indicative of the cultivation, formation, and birthing of **MESSY BeBes**! This was evidenced by my son's school perception and change in disposition, the teacher's communication and demeanor toward me as a parent, and her disinterest in any solution that supported my son's success.

These were indicators of the **MESSY BeBes** crop soon to be harvested had that matter gone undetected and inadequately addressed. I was determined, though the **MESSY BeBes** were trying to form, I was going to do everything in my power to ensure that they didn't or if they did, they would not prosper!

The unlimited possibilities, heartfelt desires, and spirited imagination we possess as children immediately and inevitably are impacted by *the process of life* and, literally before we know it, as illustrated in the above account with my son, we can form, assume, or inherit **MESSY BeBes**! Our wide-eyed, daring, and unstoppable younger selves begin to change to accommodate the soiled condition tainted by the **MESSY BeBes**. We grow to believe we no longer can do *anything* and *everything* we desire in our heart! In fact, we may even question that which we already can do.

I knew I had to address the situation presenting itself at the school. Bottom line, I requested a school meeting to include the teacher, her assistant, school social worker, school counselor, the teacher whose class my son had been moved to, and the principal – all of whom were familiar with Phillip at this point. And I had prepared for the meeting.

During the meeting I expressed my concerns as well as articulated my attempts to work with the teacher. I shared my expectations and request to have my son removed from his teacher's classroom. As I expected, Phillip was moved to the classroom of a teacher better suited to assist in his success and he began to enjoy and thrive in school again, with no further disciplinary actions. The example illustrated here is a very real and relevant one that happens all too often throughout settings everywhere.

As parents, it is vitally important we are involved and aware of our children's school environment and even more, aware of how the environment affects them. Outside of the home and direct care of primary caregivers, school environments and its personnel, starting with and including daycare, can be the most significant influences on a child's social, emotional, mental and academic development, both good and bad. After all, that is where children spend most of their waking time their first 17 years of life.

During this period of their life, core belief systems are formed. This is when individuals' identities, self-images, what they believe to be true about whom they are, and what they can do begin to manifest... moving them in the direction of their divine destiny *or* destruction.

The conception of **MESSY BeBes** does not *just* happen...just as the conception of a natural baby doesn't. **MESSY BeBes** (**M**ental, **E**motional **S**elf-**S**abotage **Y**ielding **B**eliefs and **B**ehaviors) occur as a result of actions or seeds sown (what's said, suggested, or done), whether intentional or not, by our own doing or that of others mainly during the formative years of life, birth to late teen, though primarily between three and eight.

Much like the choice to engage in the act of sex itself, though the intent is typically more for pleasure than procreation, one must realize when choosing to have sex that conception is a possible outcome. Likewise, the things we experience along our *process* of life can produce babies, **MESSY BeBes** – what we think, say, and do that take root, grow, and eventually manifest into...you name it.

When a person lives with a host of undetected or unrecognized MESSY BeBes, that person can form a distorted view of self and likely a less than optimal perspective of life; thus manifesting a life contrary to the one originally intended – the one the heart longs to fulfill.

The process of cleaning up **MESSY BeBes** can be a life-long process; however the process can get easier and happen quicker once we become aware of the existence of the **MESSY BeBes** and are willing to do what's necessary to clean them up – change. It is this apperception that can cause a shift and move a person from a pool of perpetual stagnation to a place of progression, from doubt to destiny – conversion that can realign us back on the path to realize the dreams once envisioned when we were but uninhibited, fearless, and imaginative children free and less jaded by **MESSY BeBes**.

I must admit, initially I thought it was ironic that the experience we faced with the school would happen just as I'd started working as a child and family psychotherapist. I considered it may have been a coincidence - a notion I quickly dismissed. I don't believe in coincidence. I believe and recognize it was a divine part of the design for my life – another necessary component to my *process*...and not just mine but my son's as well.

*W*e all have within us everything we need to be "successful" in life; to realize and walk in our unique purpose, the very thing that will please our heart and give us that deep sense of joy and fulfillment. We're all given a gift that is the key to our purpose and our wealthy place. That doesn't change over time; we do. I have come to believe the experiences we have along our life journey are aspects of our *process* that can and do serve to equip us for our purpose in becoming our best selves when we choose to embrace them as such.

"If you want to become the person you have the potential to be,
you must believe you can!"
~ John Maxwell[4]

The word *hope,* according to its biblical reference, conveys a "confident expectation or assurance based upon a sure foundation for which we wait with joy and full confidence."[5] There is no doubt in hope. So if there is any doubt in your mind that the life you long for can still be attained, arrest that thought! Banish it! Because you can have the life you hope for...as it aligns with the divine plan for your life!

You do not have to continue to take care of **MESSY BeBes**, in fact you should not! They need to be released! Cut off! Evicted from your mental storehouse. To allow **MESSY BeBes** (**M**ental, **E**motional **S**elf-**S**abotage **Y**ielding **Be**liefs and **Be**haviors) to stay will only continue to derail your progress toward your purpose.

It will only delay your doing those things that are necessary for you to move forward. It will continue to keep you at bay from that which you secretly desire in your heart, keeping you simply living outside the possibilities. Your **MESSY BeBes** must be dealt with and you are the only one who can release and let go of them.

"If most of us remain ignorant of ourselves, it is because self-knowledge is
painful and we prefer the pleasures of illusion."
~ Aldous Huxley[6]

Are you willing to identify and do what is necessary to release your **MESSY BeBes**? Are you willing to do the work to rid yourself of them? Are you ready to emancipate yourself and be free to believe for what you really want versus what you have convinced yourself to settle for?

If you're really ready, then let's go! Do it now! No more just thinking about it. That won't do it. Famed psychologist and television show host, Dr. Phil McGraw has said, "The universe rewards action. Successful people take action towards a known outcome. You can't think about it. You have to do it – and you don't do it for a week or a month. You do it until. Until you get what you want!"

To begin to change your life you must change what you think and honestly believe that has kept you from what you want. The sooner you do the better! But be warned! You may have decided to take action to release your **MESSY BeBes** but know they yearn to stay latched on to you. They are like blood-sucking leeches; clinging to you for their survival, their own personal gain while sucking the very life out of you, giving nothing beneficial in return. They keep you exhausted, busy with hamster wheel gymnastics, running reckless and nonstop through your mind.

Think of it this way; maybe you have had a friend or family member that comes for a visit and just doesn't want to leave? Initially you enjoy their company and are glad they are there. They in turn love how accommodating you are, how welcomed you make them feel, and how you just do for them.

Their visit prolongs into a 'stay'; so long in fact you begin to wonder if they have a job or anyplace else to go. Regardless, when you gently remind them that YOU DO have a job and a routine of life to get back to, they seem irritated! That's the life of the **MESSY BeBes**.

They are not going to go on their own and will not leave without some resistance. So, be ready. They will try to linger. They will try and convince you that they will not be in the way or cause a mess or whatever it is they've been telling you that have convinced you to permit them to stay. They may have presented themselves as caring and even felt protective of you or to you in the beginning, and maybe even seemed helpful at times - after all they did come along with *the process*. But you now know otherwise.

*R*ecognize them for who and what they really are and respond accordingly. **MESSY BeBes** camouflage as protectors when they are actually dream killers and destiny destroyers! I'm telling you now; to reach your desired destiny in life you must open your eyes and see them as the deceivers they really are and be intentional to get rid of them. You must accept the fact that you will feel the pain of discomfort as they latch on, not wanting to free themselves of their host – your mind!

Don't waste time blaming them for wanting to hang out with you. Your mind is an abundant, wealthy place not just for you, but for everyone or thing attached to you! But it is not profitable – in your best interest - to have just anything and everyone attached to you.

As you prepare for the process or operation to be free of your blood sucking **MESSY BeBes** leeches you must be sure to go through pre-op! Pre-op is the procedure prior to an operation to prepare for surgery. In this case, pre-op may resemble:

- your first making a decision as to what needs to be removed from you / your life,

- being committed to the process / operation,

- being intentional to solicit the support or your key people that they will make sure you show up for your appointment, a next step toward your goals / purpose.

After pre-op, it's time for the operation. As it is in the natural, you can expect to feel some pain, and possibly see a little blood with the detachment of the leeches. This blood is an indicator of what has taken place, a severing. Detachment. Separation. And with time, support, encouragement and the love of your support people your post-op healing, restoration and continued growth will begin!

But it all has to begin with your decision. So, decide! Remember whose house it is...Yours! Take authority! Let those **MESSY BeBes** know, their time is up! They are no longer welcomed and they are of no good use to you! They do not serve you in reaching your destiny! They are parasites that have to be released, leeches that have to be cut off, and removed. Over-extended visitors who have to go! There is no more room for them in your house! Bye-bye!

"The purpose of empowerment is to urge you towards freedom, to help each of you to break free of all limitations. It is that freedom that will give you eternal happiness and finally connect you with the unconditional realization of TRUTH."

~ Steve Maraboli[7]

Anything that limits who you are, limits what you are created to do, and anyone who agrees or participates in those limits is a hindrance to your fulfilling your purpose. Change has to occur to bring about the proper alignment for the fulfillment of that which you seek. For the sake of your purpose, you must choose to let go of the limiting beliefs, enabling mindset, and counterproductive behaviors. You must be committed to the process of change and as needed, seek wise counsel or professional help.

Do not continue to entertain any limits in your life that keeps you outside of your place of prosperity, the place of wholeness, health, wealth, mental and emotional freedom, spiritual growth, and maturity. The choice is yours. The decision to become who you need to be in order to live the life you desire will likely be easier than the *process* you will encounter along the way.

"If you plan on being anything less than you are capable of being, you will probably be unhappy all the days of your life."

~ Abraham Maslow[8]

Chapter 4

Choices

"Defining myself, as opposed to being defined by others, is one of the most difficult challenges I face."
~ Carol Moseley Braun[1]

Ponder this. Life is the journey which equips us to function and flow in our gift, talents, and abilities to help others as we fulfill our ultimate purpose. Within that, we have free will – the ability to make choices that are consistent with what we desire, realizing we will own full responsibility for the consequences.

I want you to go with me on a little journey. A journey you may have forged once upon a time but perhaps abandoned a while ago. I first want to prepare you so you can really explore and enjoy this quick journey. Let's begin by relaxing our mind and body as much as possible.

EXERCISE: If you're not already, get in a comfortable, relaxed position where you're free of as many distractions as possible. Isolate yourself and remove any physical barriers, noise, etc. that may cause you to be preoccupied or unable to focus. Again, you may not be able to eliminate all obstacles or hindrances at the moment but do the best you can. You can always come back and do this again later. Now, begin by taking a long, deep breath in through your nose for a count of five, and then exhale slowly blowing gently through your mouth for a count of five. Let's do that again...take a deep breath in for a count of five, then exhale for a count of five. Feel free to do it again if you'd like to help clear your mind of any chatter so you can really focus on this next section. Now using your childlike, uninhibited imagination, I want you to take a few moments to imagine your ideal life. Pause your reading here until you have completed imagining, but take your time and really allow yourself to experience it.

Now that you're done I want you to grab pen and paper and honestly answer the following questions with your most immediate unfiltered responses.

- Where do you see yourself living? Picture it!
- Describe the house you live in, the immediate surroundings, and the community.
- What vehicle(s) do you own? What is the year of the vehicle? Color? Features?
- What do you do to earn income? Do you have a job? Are you an entrepreneur? Both?
- Are you married? Describe your spouse.
- Do you have children? If so, what are their gender and ages?
- Do you live close to family? How often do you see them?
- Do you travel? For business? Pleasure? Both?

- How many vacations do you take each year? Destinations? What type of accommodations do you secure for your vacation? For how long?

- Do you attend or belong to a church or religious organization?

- Do you volunteer your time or services to a charitable organization?

- Do you fluently speak a foreign language?

- Who are your friends? Are they the ones you have today?

- What else did you imagine or would like to add?

How does your ideal, imagined life compare to the reality you live today? How closely aligned are they? What things would need to be different for you to have what you imagined? Do you believe you can still have at least some of what you saw when you truly allowed yourself to imagine? As Henry Ford once said, "Whether you think you can or you think you can't, you're right!"

"Whatever you decide, don't let it be because
you don't think you have a choice."
~ Hannah Harrington[2]

What we do with our lives and the opportunities presented, or even the opportunities we create, is our choice. Our choices are what we do, the action we take regarding a thing based on what we think and believe to be true!

*O*ften, most people take a passive, reactive role in creating the life they live. They tend to simply allow things to happen and then react to or reflect on the outcomes as though the outcomes were by chance and somehow outside of their control. The actuality is that the condition of much of our lives is in direct correlation to the collective choices we've made over time.

Even when someone chooses not to make a proactive decision regarding a particular situation, the act of **not** making a decision is itself a decision and that person is still exercising their choice. That is known as a passive or reactive decision; nevertheless, it is a decision that produces consequences.

"The difference between where we are and where we want to be is created by the changes we are willing to make in our lives."

~ John Maxwell[3]

We all are born with a gift or gifts, certain abilities, and talents. We can use our gifts and abilities and develop the skills necessary to make happen in our life what we were created for, yet, too few people actually do. Why is that? One primary reason I think many people live far below that which they could have is because they experience **life** in a way which causes them to stop believing that they **can**.

They stop believing in themselves. The voice of that little boy or girl who once proclaimed so many hopes and dreams has now been ushered into silence. They become afraid of failure and, remarkably, success! Sadly, some just simply give up during their *process* and become comfortable with their chosen plight, which leaves them frustrated and unfulfilled.

What about you? Have you allowed life to quench your hopes, aspirations, and passions? Have you allowed life to overwhelm you or have you taken control of it? Do you believe you really are subject to the life you have? Have you resolved yourself to the notion that your life is not going to change or do you believe there is and can be more for you? As long as you have hope there is the possibility for change. You can change and you **must** change if you want your life to change!

The condition of much of our lives is in

direct correlation to the collective choices

we've made over time.

People who resign themselves to a life unfulfilled are often stuck in a place called "comfort". In other words, they fail to realize that an extended residence in a comfort zone is always oversaturated with the *average* and really is the beginning of their demise.

"Whether you are a success or failure in life has little to do with your circumstances; it has much more to do with your choices."
~ Nido Quebein[4]

Why is there no production in a comfort zone? Because it is the state in which people feel "safe, at ease, and void of provocation", which is the definition of comfort itself. Being comfortable sounds ideal, right? This is what people tend to believe they are striving for in life – a place where everything is "nice and easy". While comfort certainly has its place in our existence, it is not a space for us to occupy for a significant period of time. It is there, in the comfort zone where dreamers are lulled into a state of complacency and in time their dreams and aspirations fade and eventually die. This is also where people live to just exist.

There is an anonymous quote which states, "A comfort zone is a beautiful place, but nothing grows there". As you think about your life, are any of your dreams still alive? Are any on life support and need to be resuscitated? Or, have you allowed any of them to die?

"You never change your life until you step out of your comfort zone; change begins at the end of your comfort zone."
~ Roy T. Bennett[5]

One of the most challenging things for a lot of people is to admit they need help and then to seek it, especially as it pertains to personal change. Many of my therapy clients have acknowledged that seeking the services of a professional counselor or therapist has been the most challenging thing they feel they've ever had to do and most assuredly it required their stepping outside of their comfort zones. I commend them for their courage in having taken the step, for many more people do not, for various reasons. Still, it is only when we accept and take responsibility for our lives that we are then in position to begin to change what we don't like about it.

"Nobody is beyond change! It may take a long time for them to do so, but it can happen."
~ Joyce Meyer[6]

Far too many people live to just exist, which is not living at all. **Living** is a present state of being. It is active. In motion. Happening now. Not waiting for then, when, or the future. It denotes movement. Growth. And it requires Faith. Are you living? Are you currently doing those things that move you toward that ideal life you imagined which cause you to feel and be alive? Are you experiencing those things that stretch you beyond your comfort zone?

One of the most challenging things for a lot

of people is to admit they need help and

then to seek it, especially as it pertains to

personal change.

Remember those childhood dreams you espoused before *life* happened? Can you still recall that feeling you felt when you believed you could do, be, and have anything you wanted and dared the world to try to stop you? Even as those thoughts flashed across your mind just now, you may have experienced a flutter of excitement at what you thought was once possible, whereas now it may seem fleeting at best.

I'm sure we all have "been there, done that" (i.e., settled in a place of comfort for a while) in some area of our life. And though the excitement of the possibilities may have dulled, it is still possible for it to be reignited. Set a fire of hope and stir it up so that you truly become alive again! Come alive in a way that propels you into your next level of *process* that is necessary for you to grow! Stretch beyond your comfort zone and open the very gifts within to achieve your dreams!

"Get comfortable being uncomfortable. Get confident being uncertain. Don't give up just because something is hard. Pushing through challenges is what makes you grow."
~ Jules Marcoux[7]

Stretched

Sometimes it's during life's situations when we are forced beyond our comfort zone that we realize we have a deep inner strength which can push us forward. When confronted with fear, we find that we have a level of courage that clothes us like a fitted glove. And through it all we hold on to faith, steadfast to the expected end, of what seemed to be the impossible.

That practically sums up most of the people I am privileged to serve in my counseling practice. There are many of them who bravely face life's challenges and make the choices that pull them out of their comfort zones and stretch them to their next level of greatness.

"Being challenged in life is inevitable, being defeated is optional."

~ Roger Crawford[8]

Set a fire of hope

and stir it up

so that you

truly become

alive again!

Chapter 5

Influences

"The past influences everything and dictates nothing."
~ Adam Phillips[1]

The series of experiences we've encountered, the roads traveled, and the lessons learned are all a part of life's journey that can make us bitter or better. We get to choose. My choices didn't always lend to my becoming better, particularly when I was still in a phase of my *process* where I was yet broken.

It was only with time and my removing myself from negative, toxic environments and people (and my choosing to work on me, to heal the brokenness and to love myself) that I began to recognize the purpose of my past. That very place of pain would develop within me a strength and independence that would prove beneficial in my ability and resolve to rise above my circumstances.

I came to realize that though I wasn't responsible for all the things that had occurred *in* my life, I was still responsible *for* my life. Simply, I would have to be the one to now change whatever it was and is that I don't like about my life. I had to choose to be an active participant and embrace *my process* to change it.

"Once in a while it really hits people that they don't have to experience the world in the way they have been told to."

~ Alan Keightley[2]

We can be aware of the need to change our condition or life circumstance and be motivated to do something about it, yet not be fully aware of just how to change it. That's where I found myself as a young single mom, and that was part of the impetus that lead me to graduate school to do what I now do – help equip and support people to change.

That very place of pain

can develop an inner strength

that proves beneficial in

your ability and resolve

to rise above your circumstances.

*T*here are several models or "stages of change"[3], yet they all contain the same fundamental elements: acknowledging an issue, desiring or intending to do something to change that issue, taking action steps to create a change in behavior, and engaging consistency to maintain the new desired behavior. Even as we take steps toward the desired change progressing in the right direction, we must keep in mind there will still be more that we must learn.

Les Brown

Leslie Calvin Brown, also known as Mamie Brown's baby boy, as he affectionately refers to himself, is best known as Les Brown and one of the best and most notable motivational speakers there has been. He was born in a low-income section of Miami, Florida, along with his twin brother. They were given up within weeks of their birth and soon thereafter adopted by a 38-year-old, unmarried cafeteria cook and domestic worker. By all accounts, it was not a good situation and the odds of Les rising above his circumstances were not in his favor.

In his 1992 bestseller book *Live Your Dreams*, Brown shares his adventures as a child including his academic struggles. Having been a poor student, mainly due to issues of inattention and restlessness (what would likely be diagnosed and labeled today as ADHD – Attention Deficit Hyperactivity Disorder), Brown was labeled "educably mentally retarded" in the fifth grade.

He could have easily resolved himself to be just that and become a "statistic", where no one outside of his immediate community would ever know his name. But obviously that was not to be his story. Despite his childhood circumstances, he decided to change his life trajectory.

Like Brown, thousands of children are born into situations every day where they may experience impoverished, desperate, neglectful or even abusive childhoods, which can and will certainly influence their life choices. However, one's past does not have to dictate one's future.

In Brown's case, his mother and a high school teacher significantly influenced the outcome of his life choices. This teacher outright refuted Brown's acceptance of the label he'd been given in school–a label that had influenced the way Brown at one time saw himself.

"Someone's opinion of you doesn't have to become your reality."

~ Les Brown[4]

That was the statement his teacher declared that dismantled Brown's perception of his previously accepted disability and limiting self-image.

Brown credits the strength and character of his adoptive mother for being his greatest inspiration to change his life which did not allow the circumstances of his past to become his story. As I said before, one teacher in particular was instrumental in his charting a different course in life. Both that teacher and his mother believed in him. They were voices that spoke life over him. They were the ones who encouraged him into his potential until it became his reality and surpassed his past.

"The purpose of influence is to speak up for those who have no influence."
(Pr.31:8) It's not about you."
~ Rick Warren[5]

Brown could have been subject to become a "product of his (physical and academic) environments". Yet, it was the strong, unrelenting influences of others that helped develop a different mental environment – a mindset that allowed him to rise above all of that.

His mother, teacher, and perhaps the acts of others and their shared faith and belief in him demonstrate how early influences shape one's perspective, self-image, and reality as they did his. It is an example of how life experiences are internalized as "truth" based on our perceptions, perspectives, and beliefs. These internalized truths ultimately guide our choices to create for us our reality of life.

"But until a person can say deeply and honestly, "I am what I am today
because of the choices I made yesterday," that person cannot say,
"I choose otherwise."
~ Stephen R. Covey[6]

As is the case with most people, Brown had a multitude of early influences –
some good, some bad, some positive and some negative. He lived in
circumstances such that both realities were possible as his future and like every
individual, he had to choose. He had to decide what he wanted for his life,
choose a pathway to lead him in that direction and then take the necessary steps
to create his desired end, making whatever adjustments along the way.

He chose to grow through and overcome obstacles he faced. He was relentless
in his *process*. Ultimately Brown's thoughts and focus, belief, decisions and
action steps toward the more positive than negative options in his life resulted
in the outcome of his story as we know it today. He defied the odds and
limitations before him.

*"You can't change where you came from, but you can change where you go
from here."*

~ Sarah Addison Allen[7]

o everything there is an opposite. In order for there to be an up,
there has to be a down; for there to be a right, there must be a left;
for there to be love, there must be hate. John Steinbeck wrote,
"What good is the warmth of summer, without the cold of winter to give it
sweetness." The very definition of a thing is what helps to conversely define its
opposite.

The essence of Brown's beginning and the impact of his early influences and
deliberate choices paved the way to his **success** story. His story is an

illustration of how what could have been a negative, stereotypical life journey was intentionally changed to its opposite. Are your choices leading you to your success story?

"You are not the victim of the world, but rather the master of your own destiny. It is your choices and decisions that determine your destiny."
~ Roy T. Bennett[8]

Many people grow up in less than favorable circumstances. Perhaps they were disadvantaged financially and experienced poverty, too little food, inadequate or unstable housing, drug addicted parents, bullying at school, domestic violence or chronic community unrest, abuse, or neglect. You may have been one who was impacted by one or several such vices.

Whatever the case, we all can probably recount some type of personal, relatable story. So why do some people seem to overcome their circumstances, at least to some degree to live relatively "successful" lives, while others seemingly can not?

You must realize and accept the fact that

though you may not be responsible

for all of the things that have

occurred in your life, you are

still responsible for your life.

Brown suggests, "Too many of us are not living our dreams because we are living our fears. A lot of people are content with their discontent. In other words, the people who can't seem to rise above to overcome their life situations lack the tools, knowledge, desire, or consistency necessary to change to the point of a true transformation".

Is that you? Are you living the vision within your heart or one that someone else defined for you? Are you making choices that reflect your hopes or those which result from your fears? Are you willing to challenge your circumstances, defy the odds and live by faith? Are you willing to invest the time and resources to develop yourself and transform your life?

Brown is someone who made a deliberate, unapologetic decision that he would not be content in his discontent. He wanted more than it appeared his life circumstances offered; so, he asked questions, studied, learned what he needed to learn, and challenged and overcame his circumstances **on purpose**. He was willing to embrace the *process - the means whereby we journey through life and attain information to become equipped and prepared to be most successful in realizing and walking in our purpose -* and be transformed.

Other people's opinions, whatever they are, do not have to become your reality. This may seem like an obvious statement, but truth be told, the contrary is exactly what many if not most people unknowingly fall prey to. If you take a minute and really examine your life, you may find that this has been true for you too, at least in some areas. I encourage you to take time for some introspection now. Here is an exercise to get you started.

Set aside time to think about and write down any areas of your life you would like to change.

It's quite possible you came to that place (what you've identified as something you want to change) because you trusted and chose to follow the suggestions, opinions or guidance of others over what you actually thought or wanted for yourself. And it likely was suggestions, opinions, or guidance from well meaning people.

Maybe you thought they knew best or maybe you believed you didn't have a choice. That was likely the case during the formative years (birth to teens) when we are heavily influenced by parents, other adult figures, older siblings, peers, the media, and society at large. It is during this developmental phase that we are being influenced and shaped in how and what we think, our beliefs, and our perspectives. Those influences impacted our subsequent decisions which in turn manifested our realities and will further go on to create our futures unless some things change.

"Influencing is just not about listening and speaking, it's the game of interpretation."

~ Harrish Sairaman[9]

Let me illustrate how the interpretation of the communication from others can have a subtle influence on an individual. This is another actual story involving my then four-year-old son, Phillip.

I was cooking dinner in the kitchen of our 2 story town house while my son watched a soccer game on television about 5 yards away. Our home had a cozy downstairs area with just enough space for him to play where I could keep an eye on him.

Out of nowhere and for no apparent reason, Phillip began to cry. Immediately I became alarmed and called out to him.

"Phillip, what's wrong?"

"I can't do that!" he sobbed as he pointed toward the television.

I was confused and a bit irritated, trying to finish up dinner so I could get to my homework. I couldn't make out what he was referencing.

I walked over and knelt beside him, asking again what was making him cry. In my mind, there was nothing in the game this active four-year old daredevil son of mine wouldn't be able to do.

Perplexed I asked, "Phillip, what's wrong? Why are you crying?" Again, he pointed at the TV and repeated himself, but this time he elaborated.

"I want to do that but I can't!" he said.

It appeared to me he was indicating he wanted to play soccer.

Still baffled I asked, "Why can't you?"

"Cause I have brown skin!" he explained.

My breath was held captive in my chest. I felt myself silently gasp! I felt sick to my stomach. I couldn't believe my ears, but there it was!

*W*hat I had intentionally worked to counter or at least minimize had found its way into our lives and exposed itself that day...right in my face! Despite my best efforts, the disparaging racial subtleties of our society which had obviously been seeded in the subconscious mind of my four-year-old had begun to sprout.

I'm not sure when or how those thoughts were planted but they evidently were there. Understanding the developmental phase he was in, understanding that his thoughts, beliefs, and perspective were still being shaped, and understanding his decisions would be impacted and future determined by all of this, my efforts intensified to make sure those corruptive seeds did not grow deeper. I worked to uproot them altogether.

"Influence is everything. One wrong influence can single handedly destroy every bit of your innocence and innocence is the root of all wisdom."

~ John Maiorana (oohGiovanni)[10]

Chapter 6

Thoughts and Beliefs

What are you thinking?

"Nothing has a greater influence over your life than your thoughts rather they are negative or positive."
~ Tasha Hoggatt[1]

Everything begins with a thought...what are you thinking?

Research suggests the average person has as many as 60,000 thoughts per day! That's absolutely mind-bogging! Obviously, we can't and don't actually process all of those daily thoughts but just the fact of the matter hints at the magnitude of the mind. So, what exactly constitutes a thought? Thought is defined as:

"an idea, opinion, notion, view, impression, judgment, assessment or conclusion produced by thinking or occurring suddenly in the mind."

Most of our thoughts are reoccurring and sadly, most of them – (upwards of 85%) are negative. This may be one reason we are warned to guard our thoughts! A particular point of wisdom comes to mind here, "Above all else, guard your heart, for everything you do flows from it." (Proverbs 4:23)[2] What profound advice and truth!

*J*ames Allen captured the essence of this in his book titled, *As a Man Thinketh,* published in 1903, which is now a matter of public domain. It has been revised countless times. Allen describes "the power of thought...and how, in [our] own thought-world, each [of us] holds the key to every condition, good or bad, that enters into [our] life, and that, by working patiently and intelligently upon [our] thoughts, [we] may remake [our] life, and transform [our] circumstances". [3]

If people can grab hold of that and begin to apply that truth to their life, many people would live life more fulfilled. I first read this book in college yet did not understand then just how powerful and profound it was. Being young and focused on "doing my thing", I had no clue of the treasure that was in my hands or how it could have set me on a different path sooner had I really studied and applied its contents. I am so thankful each day brings new opportunity!

*"I did then what I knew how to do. Now that I know better,
I do better."*

~ Maya Angelou[4]

My people are destroyed for lack of knowledge. (Hosea 4:6)[5]

Understanding the power of our thought life and taking control of it is key. Many of us go through life not understanding why we continue to do the very things we do not want to do. We can have the best intentions when we start a thing and will give it our most sincere efforts. Still, we can end up on the other side, not having accomplished the desired outcome. But why is that?

As we go through life working to accomplish goals and striving toward certain outcomes, we may (as we should) take time to examine the way we have gone about achieving our goal; consider where things might have gone wrong or even ponder what we can do differently the next time. These are definitely valid points of consideration and should be addressed.

Unfortunately, there is often times the inclination to look more so at *what we do* than *why we do*. Our "*why*" is too influential of a factor to go unexamined. If we stop at just considering *what we do* and don't go deeper to the *why we do*, we will misaim our attention, misappropriate our focus, and miss getting to the root of the matter.

I work with people who seek my services because they want to experience some type of change in their life, be it mood, relationships, or goals. Typically, by the time they reach out to someone in my field, they've tried all they know to do. I'm honored to be able to help those I serve. I understand that the "presenting problem", (the reason they've determined they come to see me for help), is rarely the real problem or issue that needs addressing. That's because *the presenting problem* may manifest in our conscious thoughts; however, the actual issues (and answers or resolutions being sought) go much deeper, for it is embedded in the person's belief system.

"Reality is a projection of your thoughts or the things you habitually think about."

~ Stephen Richards[6]

"Cognitive-behavioral therapy (CBT) is a form of psychotherapy that treats problems and boosts happiness by modifying dysfunctional emotions, behaviors, and thoughts. Unlike traditional Freudian psychoanalysis, which probes childhood wounds to get at the root causes of conflict, CBT focuses on solutions, encouraging patients to challenge distorted cognitions (thoughts) and change destructive patterns of behaviors."[7]

In the world of psychology and the practice of CBT, there is a principle represented by this formula:

$$A + B = C$$

I like this formula because it is a simple enough tool for my clients or anyone to remember and employ readily. I'll expound a bit. *A* represents an action, thought or experience, *B* represents someone's belief (whether rational or irrational) regarding "A", and *C* represents the resulting conclusion or choice. The depth of this principle should not get lost in the simplicity of its formula.

*W*hatever you do or experience as a result of someone's action (including your own), coupled with what you *believe* about what you do or experience will inevitably result in your choice or the conclusion drawn regarding it. In other words, it is (B), what someone believes to be true concerning (A), any event, thought or experience, that determines (C), how they will respond. We are not always in control of (A) what happens, but we are the ones who determine (B), what meaning we associate with or believe to be true about what happened.

Jonathan Leicester suggests that "belief has the purpose of guiding action rather than indicating truth."[8] We are the ones who determine or assign the meaning to what we experience; therefore, it is what we impose as **true** in any given situation that determines how we will respond to it. This in turn leads to how we choose to respond, what we choose to do. The key here is this: the factor that most impacts the choice someone makes or the conclusion someone draws about a thing is what they believe to be true about it. That said, (B) Belief, is the key.

Maybe you've heard it said this way, "whatever you think about, you bring about" (cause it to occur in your life). George Carlin said it this way, "The reason I talk to myself is because I'm the only one whose answers I accept."[9] No matter how that formula is articulated, it comes down to this, you have the power to think a thing into existence based on what is rooted in your belief system.

This makes it vitally important to know or at least have some awareness of how we come to believe that which we believe...how our beliefs are formed, culminating into a belief system. It is out of our belief system, which is within our subconscious mind, that we make the choices and draw the conclusions that create our lives, our realities, and the life we each live.

PRACTICE: Read the following sentences. Which ones do you agree with?

I am skinny.

I don't need a lot of money.

I am fat.

I am pretty.

It's okay to stretch the truth to get what you need.

Black people are dangerous.

I don't do well in math.

Don't tell family secrets.

The USA is the best country in which to live.

With Christ, all things are possible.

Men often think about sex.

Bad things always happen to me.

If I had more money, I'd be happier.

I have to be wary of people who don't look like me.

I can't live without _____ (you fill in the blank).

These statements represent more than someone's thoughts or opinions. They are actual beliefs! Try to articulate why you believe and agree with the ones you do. Use the A + B = C formula. Again, (A) is an action, experience, thought; (B) is what you believe about (A), and (C) is what you conclude or choose to do as a result. I'll use the first sentence, *I am skinny,* to illustrate how the formula plays out, even without our awareness, and more specifically for me, how it played out in my life.

Growing up, I was always told I was skinny (A = my experience). As a little girl I had long arms, long thin legs, and even had a long neck. Now some may think, "What's wrong with that?" while others may not find those characteristics appealing. As for me being in a family where most females were of medium build or larger, I was more of the exception.

The tone and context in which the skinny reference was made was often in relation or contrast to others who clearly were not. In fact, not only was I told that I was (and actually was) skinny, but it was also noted that as I matured and developed, I remained skinny. With little boobs, no butt, big teeth, and big eyes, I had all the attributes that seemed unattractive and did not draw the interest of the right guys.

So, I interpreted and internalized *skinny* as something *not preferred, less desirous, and least attractive* (B = what I believed to be true about being skinny and therefore, me). That was my perception and what I continued to believe for a long time. However, interestingly enough, I don't recall anyone actually saying that I was not pretty or attractive.

The factor that most impacts

the choice someone makes or

the conclusion someone draws

about a thing is what he or she

believes to be true about it.

Contrarily, I remember people referring to me as 'cute'. Yet because of the tone and context in which I was often referenced as being skinny, I became self-conscious about my body self-image and did not feel pretty *enough* (C = consequence / conclusion). It wasn't my body size itself that lead me to think I was skinny. It was my body size and composition in relation to how it was referenced or compared to others. And as one of my good friends, mentor, and author of the foreword, Tonya Joyner-Scott, has said, "Comparison is the thief of our destiny."

Self-consciousness regarding my body-image resulted in mindful behaviors as well. I became shyer and less comfortable socially. I dressed to attract as little attention as possible. In fact, I believe that this likely led to my wanting to excel academically, to somehow compensate for what I thought I lacked in physical appeal.

Webster's Dictionary defines belief as "a state or habit of mind in which trust or confidence is placed in some person or thing". A belief is received and stored in the subconscious mind, whether it is true or false, rational or irrational, and impacts what a person does. How does that happen? The belief system is formed through the five senses: taste, sight, touch, smell, and sound. These five things are what provide the information (or evidence) that you examine to determine whether or not the information will be stored as truth for you. Whatever you choose to hold as truth then molds or shapes who you are and what you believe you can have.

Put another way, the belief system is formed by perceptions and assumptions (ideas, thoughts, or mental seeds sown) that you receive (either from your own thought life or as influenced by others) that determine who you are and what you become, in all areas of your life. As these perceptions, whether true or false, positive or negative, are accepted as truth by your subconscious mind (which cannot distinguish real from fake, truth from lie), they are sown into your belief system. To put it succinctly, they take root and become what you believe, and what you believe becomes your perception of reality. That said, **your belief system is very powerful and instrumental in creating your reality.**

*T*he more beliefs are reinforced with supporting evidence or rehearsed by constant meditation, the stronger, more hard-coded they become in the subconscious mind and therefore harder to change, thereby forming that belief system. Likewise, to the contrary; when an idea is presented along with contradicting evidence, that idea, if it makes it past the conscious filter into your subconscious, will likely not take root or if it does, it will grow weaker and can be more easily changed.

Our belief system is influenced and formed based on information from several direct and indirect sources, albeit from parents, family, friends, teachers, media, etc. These sources can suggest ideas or information that is either productive or counterproductive to our well-being. For example, because of the trusting nature and inherent dependence of children, they will immediately receive what they are told as truth. When repeated over and over it will then become their belief.

Imagine the first time you saw and were told a boy was a boy, a dog was a dog, a car was a car, the stove was hot, water was wet, the sun defined 'day', the outdoor darkness was 'night', etc. You didn't think to question what you were told. You didn't consider whether it was true or not. You believed it was, and so it remained, a truth, unless or until there was alternative information presented that caused you to reconsider what you believed. This same concept can be applied in ways that can have adverse effects as well. Such was the case, though unintentional I'm sure, with me and the way I was constantly referenced as skinny, even being called Olive Oil (the girlfriend of the cartoon character Pop Eye) by peers during my teen years.

Similarly, if a child is constantly told that she is stupid, can't do certain things, and always gets into trouble, those statements will likely become her truth. And though the statements may very well be based in false evidence, they still can become her self-fulfilling prophecies (becoming real or true by virtue of having been predicted or expected).

Here, the child would likely develop a low self-esteem and poor self-image. If a teacher, family member, or friend comes along and says otherwise (i.e. tells her she is smart, she can learn, she can do anything, people like her, and want to be around her, etc.) the child most likely wouldn't believe them, especially if the negative information is being communicated more often than the positive and if it's being communicated by someone in a position of authority.

The child would be less likely to receive the positive messages as truth because we **act** based on what it is we *believe* to be true, not necessarily based on what is said, whether it is true or not. As explained using my own personal example, no one ever said I wasn't attractive because I was skinny. But based on what was said and the context in which it was communicated, it shaped what I *believed* to be true about it; which was I was skinny and skinny was not what those around me preferred.

We all are influenced very early in life by the ideas and beliefs of others that we unconsciously (without being aware of, giving thought to or consideration) adopt as our own. It's only as we grow and begin to experience life, and have ideas of our own which create a sense of dissonance, that we may be stirred to consider change.

Webster defines dissonance as "lack of agreement; the *dissonance* between the truth and what people want to believe; especially: inconsistency between the beliefs one holds or between one's actions and one's beliefs." When this state exists, it creates opportunity for us to:

- examine a particular belief,
- challenge the evidence that supports or contradicts that belief,
- consider other information, and
- make a *decision* to keep or release what we believe.

I had what I believe to be a revelation while writing one day. The idea came to me; *you don't have to work to change a belief. You choose to release or receive a belief, by faith.* It's that simple. Choose. It's a matter of a decision. It is only after you have chosen what it is you will believe that you then engage *work*. Work is the definitive action or steps you take to align your behavior with the chosen belief.

And herein lies a reason I believe some people choose to hold on to old, non-productive or simply irrational beliefs – they do not want to change their behavior. They value the rewards of their current behavior more than the perceived value or required discipline associated with the process to truly change.

"One of the greatest regrets in life is being what others would want you to be, rather than being yourself."

~ Shannon L. Alder[10]

Depicted in the award-winning film, The Help, here is another example of how thoughts and beliefs shape our consciousness:

"The first time I was ever called ugly, I was thirteen. It was a rich friend of my brother Carlton's over to shoot guns in the field.

'Why you crying, girl?' Constantine asked me in the kitchen.

I told her what the boy had called me, tears streaming down my face.

'Well? Is you?'

I blinked, paused my crying. 'Is I what?'

'Now you look a here, Egenia'-because Constantine was the only one who'd occasionally follow Mama's rule. 'Ugly live up on the inside. Ugly be a hurtful, mean person. Is you one a them peoples?'

'I don't know. I don't think so,' I sobbed.

Constantine sat down next to me, at the kitchen table. I heard the cracking of her swollen joints. She pressed her thumb hard in the palm of my hand, something we both knew meant Listen. Listen to me.

'Ever morning, until you dead in the ground, you gone have to make this decision.'

Constantine was so close, I could see the blackness of her gums.

'You gone have to ask yourself, Am I gone believe what them fools say about me today?'

She kept her thumb pressed hard in my hand.

I nodded that I understood. I was just smart enough to realize she meant white people. And even though I still felt miserable, and knew that I was, most likely, ugly, it was the first time she ever talked to me like I was something besides my mother's white child. **All my life I'd been told what to believe about politics, coloreds, being a girl.** But with Constantine's thumb pressed in my hand, **I realized I actually had a choice in what I could believe.**"

~ Kathryn Stockett[11]

Simply put, at some point in life you not only have the option to "make up your own mind" about what you do, but you come into the realization that you have a choice in what you actually accept as 'your truth'. You have a choice in what you believe.

I would offer it's at that point you have the responsibility to gain a *conscious awareness* of what you actually believe. This is imperative to understand and do because it will be instrumental in your creating an authentic, congruent life. Most people begin to reflect on this concept more vividly once of majority age, when outside of the physical and financial responsibility and control of their parents or caregivers, if not before.

You take ownership, responsibility for *your* life by doing the things *you* choose to do, that align with *your* beliefs, *your* desires, *your* purpose and plans! In order to do that, you must be cognizant of what those actually are. Now coming into that knowledge and actually doing the things you really desire, particularly once you're no longer a dependent may be easier said than done, because the mind you now have has been influenced for years by your experiences, various people, and their ideas and beliefs.

You may now be in a space where you become more cognizant of the fact that all the things you were told or even thought you believed earlier in life, may not be true for you now. Though you recognize you can act independently of your parents' desires or plans for you (or those of others), you may not make that transition as readily.

You may want to; may even tell yourself you're going to, but you notice you just aren't taking the steps you thought you would. Why? Most likely it's because what you *think* you believe and what you *actually* believe are not one in the same; they are different. This difference is an indication there are things you think and therefore believe that need to change if you're going to move toward what it is you *say* you want, versus that which you believe you can have.

There has to be a change in the things you think in order for your thoughts to become new beliefs which reflect your true desires. And the process of your changing your mind for that transformation to occur will only happen when approached **deliberately**. You have to become aware or conscious to "think about what you are thinking about", which in turn determines what you come to believe and act upon. This process is what will then create real change in your life. So, at any point you decide you want to change, it is your responsibility to change!

"The world as we have created it is a process of our thinking.
It cannot be changed without changing our thinking."

~ Albert Einstein[12]

Chapter 7

Power of the Mind

The Mind: A beautiful servant or a dangerous master

~ Osho[1]

We know that things begin with a thought and thoughts originate in the mind. The mind is extremely complex and there are varying theories and approaches to understand its complexities; still, for the sake of this reading, it is important that we have a working knowledge of how it functions. The mind consists of the conscious and unconscious, which also includes the subconscious. While most people have heard of these systems, fewer are aware of just how they function. I'll offer a brief overview here with the main focus being on the subconscious mind.

The conscious mind is probably what most people reference when they think of or talk about "the mind". The conscious mind is the part of the mind that attributes to our "awareness'; it has no memory and can only hold or entertain one thought at a time. Because of how the mind at large works, how quickly it processes and causes responses, and its functions, it can seem as if the conscious mind holds more than just one thought at a time, but it does not.

The conscious mind serves to identify incoming information, compare that information to stored information and previous experiences, analyze the collective information, and then it decides what to tell you to do. This decision is instantly sent to your subconscious mind as a message to retrieve the corresponding behavior (based on what was processed by the conscious mind) which it does, and the resulting behavior is then exhibited. Essentially, you act out or display what your subconscious mind has been told to do. This is actually contrary to what most people readily perceive and believe.

Most people believe what they think, what they do, and how they make decisions comes from their conscious mind. This is not the case. Most research supports the fact that our behavior and decisions originate at a subconscious level. Generally, our conscious mind issues the commands while our subconscious simply obeys by retrieving what is asked of it. So, it will *appear* when we are making decisions that we are doing so with our objective, conscious mind; yet what we are really experiencing is the **result** of the conscious mind *rationalizing, explaining, or making sense* of the decisions made by our subconscious mind. People are unaware of this process because it is unconscious. Does that surprise you? You may need to read that a few more times and really let it sink in.

*M*ost researchers agree 95% of our behavior and decisions are controlled by the subconscious mind.[2] That is amazing and almost incomprehensible. It shows just how powerful the subconscious is. Herein lays the importance of being **intentionally** mindful of what is allowed to be programmed in your mind.

Brian Tracy is recognized as a personal success authority in the world today. He has extensively studied the mind, human behavior and how to help people become successful. He, along with research scientists and psychology professionals agree that the mind, particularly the subconscious mind is the key to changing behavior. **The subconscious mind is noted to be at least 30,000 times more powerful than the conscious mind and is believed to be the most important part of the mind.**[3]

Unlike the conscious mind, the subconscious mind is subjective, does not process negatives, and is at work twenty-four hours a day, seven days a week. It is always on and is **always** absorbing, recording, and storing information whether you want it to or not. It never shuts off! Think about that! Everything you have ever heard, seen, tasted, smelled, touched, or felt in your emotions has been processed and stored in the subconscious part of the mind – your memory bank.

Our subconscious does not delineate

or know the difference between

what is true or false,

real or fake; it accepts all things

as truth, whether true or not.

Think of the subconscious as a master computer. It puts out (cause you to do) what's been put into it (what you have thought, said and believe). It can not create or generate anything outside of what it has already received. It solely does as it's told by your conscious mind. This is why you may have heard the saying 'guard what you allow to enter your gateways – what you see, hear, touch, smell, and taste – because it will likely be stored in your subconscious, thereby influencing your decisions...and this can work for or against you.

"The mind can start to work in your favor or against you at any given time. It's a matter of turning your thoughts and beliefs around."

~Edmond Mbiaka[4]

To say the subconscious mind is powerful is still yet an understatement. Just think, it is the subconscious that controls and regulates our involuntary body functions; things we do yet give no thought to every second of every day; the regulation of our body temperature, breathing, walking, sleeping, bending of joints, limbs, etc. Can you imagine if we had to stop and literally think about actually doing just one of these things? We would not be able to do much of anything else!!!

If you think of the subconscious mind as the storehouse of your life, it is where you will find a vault of information about you, even that which was stored there before you were even conscious or aware of it: your thought life, memories, habits, feelings, preferences, comfort zones, behaviors, and patterns. It's these patterns you've established as a response to your life experiences that comprise your subconscious programming. And these patterns or habits are what allow people who know you to somewhat "predict" what it is you will likely say and do.

We become creatures of habits and certain habits are oftentimes displayed as **MESSY BeBes** which take residence in our subconscious. We already know **MESSY BeBes** are not going anywhere willingly or easily as we become accustomed to them being a resident of our comfort zone. So, it should not surprise you that when you attempt to do anything outside of that comfortable zone, you feel a sense of being upset, discontent, awkward, or possibly even fearful.

*W*hatever the feeling might be **it is just an indicator that you are doing something *unknown* or *unfamiliar* to your subconscious.** The subconscious has no stored reference of the "new or different" information it is now receiving and **that** causes you to feel as if something is wrong. But, not so! It's just the opposite.

Be encouraged! Don't give in, give up, or turn back because of that feeling or any thought that may come to suggest you should. Though that feeling may cause a temporary feeling of *dis-ease*, know that as you persist and press through, continuing to do the 'new' thing, over time will become **known** (to the subconscious) and bring about the anticipated change – a new behavior which will be that which moves you in the direction you desire.

That's how new habits start to form. I'm sure you may have heard that if you do the same thing consistently for at least 21 days, it will create a habit. Any habit you currently have started with a thought that you acted upon and continued to do or reinforce over and over and over again, until it became that habit. It took time to form, which is one reason habits can be difficult to change. The same consistent action and time needed to create your current habits, when trying to change them, will require the same, intentional, deliberate type of actions done repeatedly over time, until the behavior becomes habit, therefore reprogramming the subconscious mind. In *Think and Grow Rich*, what is perhaps the best single book ever written on personal success, Napoleon Hill writes, "If you fail to plant DESIRES in your subconscious mind, it will feed upon the thoughts which reach it as the result of your neglect."[5]

Knowing that, it stands to reason then that we would need to willfully engage consistent, deliberate actions to change the thoughts and those things about us that we do not like or that are counterproductive to our goals. When in reality, the subconscious mind is something most people take little to no time to *understand, intentionally influence or change*, yet it plays **the** most significant role in determining our very outcomes in life.

95% of our

behavior and decisions

are controlled by

the subconscious mind.

Think about this: how many times have you wanted to change something in your life? Yet no matter your best efforts, you didn't or felt you just couldn't? Maybe you changed your mind and talked yourself into believing you really didn't want it or for whatever reason you couldn't have it; so, you gave up *in the process* before achieving the desired outcome. This scenario plays out daily, perhaps several times a day, in most people's lives, in one area or another. It could occur in a small, seemingly unimportant area of your life, but repeated over time becomes a habit. A habit of quitting, giving up, or settling – a programming or training of the mind.

"We become what we repeatedly do."

~ Sean Covey[6]

Though most people may not understand the power of the subconscious mind or invest the time, resources, and necessary consistency to retain or change its "programming", the power and importance of this is exemplified in the worlds of mass media and business. Those arenas definitely see, believe in, and invest in influencing the subconscious mind! The multi-billions of dollars spent on marketing and advertising is tangible proof.

According to the statistics company, Statista, "The United States is, by far, the largest advertising market in the world. In 2016, more than 190 billion U.S. dollars were spent in advertising in the United States. This figure is more than double the amount spent in advertising in China, the second largest ad market in the world."[7]

Why is advertising BIG business? Corporations and business owners are aware of the buying power and they want to influence where money is spent. Each business wants you and I to spend it with them, so they spend billions of dollars in television and digital advertising (radio, magazine, outdoor, and newspaper), cinema advertising, and mobile advertising.

*T*his is called creating 'media influence'; the actual force exerted by a media message, resulting in either a change or reinforcement in audience or individual beliefs.[8] Companies invest billions of dollars in advertising to influence what you see, hear, think, and want (ultimately what you experience) in order to steer your buying decisions toward their clients' products or services. The vehicle is advertising, the method is subliminal programming of the subconscious mind.

I was not surprised to learn that the advertising revenue from Super Bowl LI in 2017 was approximately $385 million U.S. dollars, with an average 30-second advertising spot during the Super Bowl broadcast costing an estimated $5 million U.S. dollars.[9] Why do companies spend that much money for a 30-second ad? Various factors come into play but quite simply, they know large numbers of people from various demographics will be tuning in and they get to influence the buying decisions of a multitude of people in a short period of time. That is robust leverage! "It was estimated that Super Bowl-related consumer spending in the U.S. would have topped 14 billion U.S. dollars in 2017...with the average American consumer spending about 75 U.S. dollars on Super Bowl Sunday."[10] Big money is being spent to influence where we spend our dollars.

Why should that matter to you or me? Because we cannot impact or change that which we are unaware. Not only does media play a subtle but huge role in what people purchase, media also plays a significant part in influencing social norms, values, and beliefs. And this can be productive or equally as dangerous.

Our subconscious does not delineate or know the difference between what is true or false, real or fake; **it accepts all things as truth, whether true or not**. That is why is it most important that we are intentional in what we allow ourselves to hear, see, and think or meditate on, especially about ourselves.

*R*esearch informs us that most of the subconscious mind is programmed by the age of seven or eight, though there is still some programming of our subconscious mind which occurs up through the mid-teen years. Subconscious programming is how children primarily learn. A common example of this is illustrated by how we learn our primary language.

Outside of an injury to the brain, we typically do not forget our primary language and we speak it fluently without exhaustive effort. Though most people realize this is true, who really ponders how or why it is? I know I certainly didn't. Like most, I initially took it for granted and accepted it as something that just happened...it just was. Of course, we know *nothing just happens.*

If you're a parent, you probably didn't think about how you taught your children the language you speak. You likely and naturally started talking to your children, interacting and communicating with them as you would anyone, believing (unconsciously) they would just learn the language (the words and their meaning) over time through constant repetition...and most children did and still do. Likewise; thoughts, beliefs, values, and ideas are formed during this formative time of youth, similarly the same way, through constant repetition and exposure. This process creates a young person's belief system which *informs* and *forms* that youngster's perspective of self, others, and the world.

Have you ever found yourself thinking or doing something out of the blue? Well, it was not *out of the blue* at all. It had to have been retrieved from someplace and that place is your subconscious.

Now, consider the amount of time people are mindlessly exposed to television shows, commercials, digital media, advertisements, and the like, receiving whatever information being disseminated by those who control the platform, whether the information is true, harmful, necessary or not.

The National Library of Medicine and other medical research sources state that "most American children spend about three hours a day watching television. Added together, all types of screen time can total five to seven hours a day."[11] Does that sound like any children you know? Researchers agree, and I concur, that this is too much screen time, for many reasons.

*T*hese media messages play in the background of our daily existence as 'white noise' or conscious and unconscious distractions that are being absorbed into the subconscious mind. This type of mass media influence can be profound and have proven to impact social norms, values, and beliefs which in turn significantly impacts behavior, cultures, and societies. Powerful!!! When you think about it, it begs the question who is actually rearing, training, and having the most influence on this current and the next generations?

Considering the amount of time the average person is exposed to media influences, I'd dare say that today the media is probably a subtle yet pervasive influence on most belief systems – both powerful and potentially dangerous left unchecked!

"How would your life be different if...You were conscious about the food you ate, the people you surround yourself with, and the media you watch, listen to, or read? Let today be the day...You pay attention to what you feed your mind, your body, and your life. Create a nourishing environment conducive to your growth and well-being today."
~ Steve Maraboli[12]

Going back to the earlier mention of my son at four years old, the power of the media on the subconscious mind was one of the major proponents influencing his thought life; even with me being a mindful parent and my limiting his television exposure. His surmising he could not play soccer because of the lack of people who looked like him (with his skin complexion) represented on television and his lack of exposure at the time was the evidence.

Just in case you're wondering if and how I helped to change my son's mental narrative, I made sure he became vastly acquainted with Pelé and many other men of color who were remotely associated with anything in which he expressed an interest.

"If you raise your children to feel that they can accomplish any goal or task they decide upon, you will have succeeded as a parent and you will have given your children the greatest of all blessings."

~ Brian Tracy[13]

As a fun fact, I thought I'd include this here...according to Wikipedia, Pelé, the Brazilian Portuguese professional forward football (known as soccer in the USA) player was born as Edson Arantes do Nascimento. He is widely regarded as the greatest football player of all time. In 1999, he was voted World Player of the Century by the International Federation of Football History & Statistics (IFFHS). That same year, Pelé was elected Athlete of the Century by the International Olympic Committee. According to the IFFHS, Pelé is the most successful league goal-scorer in the world, scoring 1281 goals in 1363 games, which included unofficial friendlies and tour games. During his playing days, Pelé was for a period the best-paid athlete in the world[14].

"Good advertising does not just circulate information. It penetrates the public mind with desires and belief."

~ Leo Burnett[15]

*T*he media has had a huge impact in shaping, forming or modifying the public's opinions and beliefs. There is much research and many theories that support this fact. The following represent what researchers study as *media influence*.

The *social constructivist* is used to describe outcomes when "media messages are the only information source where the audience may implicitly accept the media-constructed reality."[16] The other and perhaps more relevant to this chapter is the *cultivation theory*. This theory states that "as an audience engages in media messages, particularly on television, they infer the portrayed world upon the real world."[17] Simply stated, this means that when a medium is your only or primary source of information concerning a matter, you are prone to believe what is reported by that source, whether it is true or not.

For example, when a group of people are primarily informed about another group of people by what is depicted of them on television, especially without any direct, personal information otherwise, they will likely believe what they are shown. While studying Communications in college, one of my professors had our class observe the media behavior of our local station at that time. It was found that when reporting negative information or crimes regarding African-Americans, the suspects' images were shown disproportionately more often than that of other racial groups, namely Caucasians.

This practice fostered and reinforced the negative stereotypes of African-Americans as being more violent and dangerous than other groups of people, which statistically was not necessarily true. This method of information distribution, by its inherent nature, can be and is used to misrepresent, create fear, encourage separation, and promote division amongst people.

"A mind that is stretched by a new idea or experience can never go back to its old dimensions."

~ Oliver Wendell Holmes, Jr.[18]

Why is this important to know? Because we all are being influenced, conditioned, and if not mindful, subtly controlled by what we **mindlessly** allow ourselves to be exposed to on a continual basis. In order to lessen the impact of that conditioning, we have to take prudent steps to do things to feed our minds information that is consistent with what **we**, as individuals, determine we want to receive...self-program, if you will. We must renew our minds to 'right thinking', to align with what we desire in life and know to be truth.

For example, if you are a Believer or a follower of Jesus Christ, to reprogram or train your mind to 'right thinking' means you do those things consistent with your having the mind of Christ...to think and therefore do the things as He would to please God the Father.

Don't copy the behavior and customs of this world, but let God transform you into a new person by changing the way you think. Then you will learn to know God's will for you, which is good and pleasing and perfect.

~ Romans 12:2 NLT [19]

Chapter 8

Change your mind, Change your life

"Those who cannot change their minds cannot change anything."
~ George Bernard Shaw[1]

"We are products of our past, but we don't have to be prisoners of it."
~ Rick Warren[2]

When you understand enough about how the subconscious mind works, you will be able to change most things in your life, if you choose to and do the work. In his book, *The Power of the Subconscious Mind*, Joseph Murphy writes, "within your subconscious depths lie infinite wisdom, infinite power, and infinite supply of all that is necessary, which is waiting for development and expression...The infinite intelligence within your subconscious mind can reveal to you everything you need to know at every moment of time and point of space provided you are open-minded and receptive."[3]

Similar to James Allen, Murphy says, "As a man thinks, feels, and believes, so is the condition of his mind, body, and circumstances. A technique, a methodology based on an understanding of what you are doing and why you are doing it will help you to bring about a subconscious embodiment of all the good things of life."[4]

An honest awareness of one's self

and acceptance of that truth

is the first step toward change,

for you can't change what you

don't know or don't acknowledge.

In the first chapter of the book, I offered this definition for you to consider regarding **Success:** *to realize and walk in purpose; to live life fulfilled.* I would suggest that this definition is a representation of the "embodiment of all the good things of life". And as I once read, by Rory Vaden, "Success is never owned, it's rented. And the rent is due everyday"[5], meaning, there is a cost we pay daily for the choices we make.

"Success is a choice that, once committed to, can be achieved. "

~ Gloria Mayfield Banks[6]

If you are not currently living what is defined here as a "successful" life, and it is your desire to do so, obviously you will need to change some things, the primary thing being your thought life. That is, what you think about, ponder, and the meaning you attach to your thoughts.

Up until now and throughout the book, we have explored various aspects of a person's being – their thoughts, belief system, and their actions or choices that most determine their current life.

An honest awareness of one's self and acceptance of that truth is the first step toward change, for you can't change what you don't know or don't acknowledge. You have to know, accept, and have some understanding of where you are before you can move in the direction you want to go. Otherwise, it's like expecting your GPS to get you to a specific destination without your first identifying and sharing your current location. Without first locating your current position, you can't chart an accurate path or plan to reach your desired destination or outcome.

"I think success has a lot to do with my own personal growth." [7]

"You have to know who you are to grow to your potential. But you have to grow in order to know who you are."

~ John Maxwell [8]

So, let's presume that you want change and you are ready and willing to change. I believe if I were to ask most people, they would agree there is some area in their life they would like to change; however, the majority of these same people never take the steps or are consistent to obtain the change they say they want.

What keeps someone from moving toward and experiencing what they say they want?

There could be many *answers* to this question including some we've already explored – the opinions of others, anticipating but not wanting to do the required work, the possibility of not reaching the desired goal, lack of necessary resources or support, lack of clarity or vision, and so on. Arguably, the primary **reason** people don't move toward and experience what they say they want is because of FEAR. Fear is an emotion that is evoked when there is a perceived threat or danger, often of the unknown.

Fear will keep you functioning

according to what you've

historically been programmed

and patterned to do, that which

is known to your subconscious mind.

In their book, *The Heart of Change*, John Kotter and Dan Cohen state, "Changing behavior is less a matter of giving people analysis to influence their thoughts than helping them to **see a truth** to influence their feelings. Both thinking and feelings are essential... but the heart of change is in the emotions." Simply, it is the emotion or feeling that is associated with a thought that creates its meaning and the strong hold attached which dictates how we experience that thought, which then moves one to action, or not. I suggest that your action or lack thereof is an indicator of your truth concerning a thing.

Think about this. Two people are working traditional jobs but they really desire to start their own respective business. They each had pondered it for months, maybe years but had not taken any specific steps to begin the process. Friday, they both show up for work to find out they have been laid off from their jobs! They are both frugal and have been diligent to amass a 9-month emergency savings account so there is no imminent need for concern. In addition, they also received a severance package from their company whereby they can sustain their respective households for 6 months with no additional income and without tapping into their emergency funds!

Though there is no immediate threat of a financial calamity, Person A is devastated by the layoff and over the next couple of months feels panicked to look for and secure another job. Person B on the other hand is excited and immediately sees the layoff as an opportunity to begin to plan for and start the business he had been envisioning.

Though both had thoughts of wanting a particular thing (in this scenario, the chance to start a business), when given what could have been viewed as an opportunity to pursue just that, it was the respective feeling evoked that drove their respective thoughts, beliefs, and subsequent actions to *create the change they said they wanted* or not.

*I*t is our decision how we respond to any particular thing or event based on how we choose and inevitably train ourselves to respond. We must train ourselves (our subconscious mind) to respond so that we produce the outcomes we want. John C. Maxwell reminds us in his book that, "our choices will lead to either the pain of self-discipline or the pain of regret. I'd rather live with the pain of self-discipline and reap the positive rewards than live with the pain of regret, which is something that can create a deep and continual ache within us."

The emotion of FEAR is at the root of that which is working against your desire and efforts to change a behavior, that behavior which is destined to work to keep you 'safe', in the place of familiarity. Fear will keep you functioning according to what you've historically been programmed and patterned to do, that which is known to your subconscious mind.

"I must say a word about fear. It is life's only true opponent. Only fear can defeat life. It is a clever, treacherous adversary, how well I know. It has no decency, respects no law or convention, shows no mercy. It goes for your weakest spot, which it finds with unnerving ease. It begins in your mind, always ... so you must fight hard to express it. You must fight hard to shine the light of words upon it. Because if you don't, if your fear becomes a wordless darkness that you avoid, perhaps even manage to forget, you open yourself to further attacks of fear because you never truly fought the opponent who defeated you."

~ Yann Martel[9]

When you begin to do anything different or something outside of your comfort zone, outside of your norm, that behavior will register in your subconscious as 'the unknown'; hence, here comes fear. Go ahead and expect it will happen. You may feel fear. And as you think about it with your conscious mind, so that you are aware of its likelihood and anticipate and prepare for it, it will have less of an effect on you.

Decide in advance that you will press through it and know that with time, the feeling of fear will subside. Feel the fear and do it anyway!

"Don't give in to your fears. If you do, you won't be able to talk to your heart."

~ Paulo Coelho[10]

Typically, fear is presumed to be and is often experienced as bad, debilitating, or of a detriment. Fear can manifest itself in many ways, including procrastination, anger, irritability, analysis paralysis, confusion, slothfulness, insomnia, fatigue, boredom, anxiety, hyper vigilance, nervousness, and a host of other things.

*M*aybe you've heard the word "fear" being used as an acronym for <u>F</u>alse <u>E</u>vidence <u>A</u>ppearing <u>R</u>eal. The take on fear that this acronym offers is a good example of the **MESSY BeBes** we may adopt, as discussed in an earlier chapter. I'd like to take a moment to examine this "False Evidence Appearing Real" perspective a bit closer.

The definition of the word **false** is, "not according with truth or fact; incorrect; *appearing* to be the thing denoted; *deliberately* made or meant to deceive; illusory; not actually so". Some <u>synonyms</u> for of the word false are: incorrect, untrue, wrong, erroneous, flawed, distorted, inaccurate, untruthful, fictitious, fabricated, made up, trumped up, counterfeit, fraudulent, traitorous, two-faced, double-crossing, deceitful, dishonest, untrustworthy, and untruthful.

Now let's look at the meaning of the word **evidence**. Evidence means "the available body of facts or information indicating whether a belief or proposition is true or valid; an outward sign, something that furnishes proof, something legally submitted to a tribunal to ascertain the truth of a matter". <u>Synonyms</u> for evidence are: proof, confirmation, verification, substantiation, corroboration, affirmation, attestation.

The word **appearing** means "come into sight; become visible or noticeable, typically without visible agent or apparent cause; seem; give the impression of being". Synonyms for appear are: become visible, come into view, come into sight, materialize, pop up, be revealed, emerge, surface, manifest itself, become apparent, become evident, come to light; arise, crop up.

Lastly, let's take a look at the word **real**. The definition of real is "actually existing as a thing or occurring in fact; not imagined or supposed; (of a substance or thing) not imitation or artificial; genuine; (of a person or thing) rightly so called; proper". Synonyms: actual, nonfictional, factual, real-life; genuine, authentic, bona fide, true, actual.

Evaluating the definitions of the individual words making up the acronym FEAR, I offer the following as a plausible different outlook regarding fear:

fear - *deliberately* deceitful information that *seems* or gives the impression of being genuine, authentic, and/or true but is not.

I believe this is the fear we face more often than any actual real injury or harm. This acronym based definition means that information is **only true to the extent that we <u>allow</u> it to be true.** Read that again. Really mediate to receive its truth.

"It is difficult to make the right choice if you fear choosing wrongly."
~ Roy T. Bennett[11]

This is what we need to first remind ourselves whenever fear tries to creep in and seize us. When the emotion of "fear" starts lurking around, we have to immediately recognize it for what it is and remind ourselves that "we are not given the spirit of fear, but of power and of love and of a sound mind" (2 Timothy 1:7).[12] Therefore, when we find ourselves resigning to fear, we must realize we are *choosing to receive* fear, just as we choose (even if by default) anything else we allow in our lives.

Many eyebrows may have been raised in response to the last few sentences read. Conflict between the ideologies of fear (irrational) versus a healthy respect for the possibility of danger (rational) may arise. Let me address what you may be thinking with an example. Say the object of fear is a snake. You are jogging along the wooded city greenway trail. A few feet ahead, you see a snake sunbathing on the sidewalk. This is where the decision point comes in.

A healthy respect for the possibility of danger/injury generates this self-talk: "Snake ahead...I don't know what kind it is...Possibly poisonous...If I'm bitten I could get hurt or worse...I need to proceed deliberately, watchful, and carefully" as I continue on. Fear would generate a self-talk similar to this: "Snake ahead...It will attack me...I will be bitten and injured or killed...I'd better turn back." In extreme cases fear would have the person freaking out or even passing out. A healthy respect for the possibility of danger/injury prompts us to rationally evaluate as we progress forward-even if forward involves a slight detour.

*F*ear keeps us from doing what we have set out to accomplish. It's important to know the difference between fear and a healthy respect for the possibility of danger/injury. The healthy respect for the possibility of danger/injury can also cause us to pause long enough to give our next words or actions a bit more thought...particularly when we're being reckless and impulsive or when what we've set out to accomplish is morally, ethically, or spiritually wrong. Thus, a healthy respect for the possibility of danger/injury is a positive tool.

With operating in fear, we must recognize that the emotion we are experiencing may be the very thing attempting to distract us or cause us to detour or operate in disbelief; thus, taking us from the very path in which we need to continue. You may need to yield, in the case of a healthy respect for the possibility of danger/injury, to further assess and determine a different direction; but don't give up or stop due to fear.

"I have accepted fear as part of life – specifically the fear of change... I have gone ahead despite the pounding in the heart that says: turn back...."
~ Erica Jong[13]

When fear knocks on the door of our heart, you have to make a decision how you are going to respond. Are you going to ignore it, as though you don't feel it and hope it goes away? Are you going to open the door and entertain it? Or are you going to snatch the door open, confront it, and tell it where it can go?

I ultimately prefer the latter even if it comes after some of the other options have been employed. Yes, sometimes that happens. One thing that has been helpful to me at times when facing fear is to take *some* time to understand why. As Stephen Richards suggests, "Use 'Why?' to help you follow the breadcrumbs back to the source of the problem."

Ask, "Why is fear present?" This may help you identify if and when **MESSY BeBes** are being formed or are present and need to be addressed. It can also be an indicator of what fear is trying to keep you from – your reaching your purpose.

So when you're faced with fear ask yourself, "Why am I feeling fearful, not at ease, not at peace?" This approach causes you to slow down and helps you **become more conscious or aware** of not only what you are thinking about but also your overall physical well-being. It helps you to think and act rationally versus possibly just *re*acting in a way that's not warranted. It puts you in position to **intentionally consider yourself**. What do I mean by that?

It causes you to literally, in the moment, think on what is it that you are thinking about or meditating on (thought consciousness) as well as reflect on the things you are or have been doing (from perhaps old or no longer helpful information stored in your subconscious). This step of self-reflection helps you to give thought to the very words you've been saying out loud as well as what you've been saying to yourself internally, your self-talk (are you speaking faith or fear, hope or doubt, etc).

It positions you to deliberately consider whom you've allowed in your space that has impacted and influenced you. Are these people speaking to your destiny or to your demise? Are they fueling your faith or your fears? It positions you to assess how you're feeling in your emotions and in your body, to generally do an overall "self-check". This can help identify the possible source of the *dis* ("an expression of negation", i.e. *dis*couragement, *dis*like, *dis*honor *dis*course, *dis*ease, *dis*agreement, etc.) that has or is occurring to bring on that which has brought about the fear.

In taking the time to intentionally go through this process you cast light on the situation, make it easier to identify the actual issue, and subsequently empower yourself to more readily address the fear *effectively*. This can dispel, dismantle, and eliminate any **MESSY BeBes** before they settle in or quickly identify any that are present.

Your heightened awareness, rational responses and corrective actions are deliberate choices that will build toward your creating new habits to change. It's helpful to ponder on the "why", but only long enough to take effective action.

*I*t is more important to recognize where you are, assess your current situation to chart where you want to be, and then devise a plan that includes the necessary steps to move you forward in that direction. Hence, you step out of fear and move toward your desired future. Stepping out is an *act of faith*-the opposite of what fear naturally causes one to do. Therefore, fear (that which provides *deliberately deceitful information that seems or gives the impression of being genuine, authentic, and/or true"...***BUT IT IS NOT***) is the enemy of your faith. You must make a conscious decision that when fear presents itself, and you know all too often it will, you will move forward in spite of it!

A word about changing

Change is often difficult...it's also inevitable...it's part of the *process*. Anyone who has grown, succeeded, and accomplished anything worthwhile did it being willing to go through a process of change. If there are things about your life that you do not like, you have the power within to change them. It's a matter of your decision to do so and the willpower to persevere.

It may require you learning something new, developing a skill set or talent you already have, or something else. The point is you have to own your life, accept responsibility for it as it is, and then employ a plan of action to create the life you want.

"All my life they had made choices for me, and I had resented it. Now the choice was mine, and once it was made, I would have no right to blame anyone else for the consequences. Loss of that privilege, to blame others, unexpectedly stung."

~ Megan Whalen Turner[14]

I'm reminded of a story of one of my earliest mentors and business success coaches, Gloria Mayfield Banks. Mrs. Banks was my upline National Sales Director at that time in my first (known) network marketing company, Mary Kay Cosmetics. To know Mrs. Banks is to love her and I had never met anyone like her. 'Small in stature only', she encompasses vision, determination, and strength that inspire others to defy limiting, self-defeating beliefs.

I recall first hearing her story, as only she can narrate it. She tells of the days as an IBM sales representative where mornings were spent gathering with colleagues during breaks, complaining about how tired they were. Tired of coming to the job...tired of doing the same thing...tired of not having more...tired...tired...just tired! She recounted routinely playing her part in that *tired* scenario until one day she seemed to have had an epiphany!

She woke up and realized, or maybe just decided, that she was not tired! And she made a decision to change, not only her physical environment, but most important and immediately, she changed her mindset and her focus. In fact, her exact words in response to her epiphany were, "I'm not tired! You're tired! (referring to her colleagues) I'm not tired!"

She stopped rehearsing the narrative that kept her focused on a condition and place she no longer wanted to be. She exchanged that dialogue for the clarity conversation that matched the life she envisioned, and began to think in that direction, speak life, exude energy, and focus on a new perspective.

Despite having endured ten years of domestic violence and being in the midst of a divorce (in her first marriage) with 2 small children, she decided not only was she not tired, but she was going to **live**, not just survive! And so she did. If you know of Mrs. Banks then you likely know her story. If you don't, then I'd encourage you to seek to know it.

Currently, Mrs. Banks leads a multimillion dollar organization in Mary Kay Cosmetics, and is ranked #3 in the United States and #1 for an African American. She has co-founded a motivational speaking and coaching company;

has been featured in multiple national media outlets, and her success has been documented in a case study at Harvard Business School, *Gloria Hilliard Mayfield at Mary Kay Cosmetics, Inc.*[15]

She is an example of hope, perseverance, resilience, dreams fulfilled, changed lives, and legacies. In the midst of her *process*, Mrs. Banks (previously Gloria Hilliard Mayfield) went on to marry the man of her dreams, Mr. Ken Banks, owner of his own successful company, and they share a blended family of now 4 adult children. Her life change experience was realized as she was able to:

- Identify the problem or issue to change,
- Be aware of her current response to the problem,
- Realize how she was allowing the problem to impact her,
- Decide what she wanted to be different...to change,
- Identify ways to make that happen,
- Implement a plan, action steps.

Mrs. Banks continues to inspire countless people worldwide.

"...no one understands your dream but you. Be okay with that. And don't look for the discipline, look for the desire—if the desire is strong enough, the discipline will show up. Find out what pushes your passion button. Distraction and discouragement will cross your path, because life happens. You'll need to rekindle your passion over and over."

~ Gloria Mayfield Banks[16]

Chapter 9

Now What?

"...*What happens is of little significance compared with the stories we tell ourselves about what happens. Events matter little, only stories of events affect us.*"

— Rabih Alameddine[1]

Now it's time for you to fully examine your narrative.

- What stories have you been telling yourself that have limited who you thought you were or believed you could become?
- Whose misinformed script have you been cast in where you no longer want the staring role?
- What truths do you hold that you realize are not *your* truths at all?
- What strengths do you now possess, that would not have been, had you not gone through certain life experiences?

- Do you have a better understanding of how you have come to be who and where you are?

- Equally important, do you see the impact of subsequent choices you've made throughout life?

- Do you see how who and where you are has come about primarily through what you have grown to believe about yourself and the multitude of life experiences you've had up until now, both good and otherwise?

Hopefully you can answer, "Yes" to some of these questions and expound with clarity. As you do, that signifies awareness, growth, and your becoming better equipped to create any change you desire.

- What insight have you gained regarding how you *previously* thought of your life experiences versus how you may think of them now?

- Do you better understand what your **MESSY BeBes** are and how they developed and grew, how they informed your decisions, and what beliefs you may have adopted earlier in life which no longer benefits you?

Considering all that you have just read throughout the book and any new information you may have possibly learned, know the bottom line to it all is this truth as stated by Marianne Williamson:

"Our **deepest fear** is not that we are inadequate. Our deepest fear is that we are powerful beyond measure. It is our light, not our darkness that most frightens us. We ask ourselves, 'Who am I to be brilliant, gorgeous, *talented, fabulous?' Actually, who are you not to be? You are a child of*

God. Your playing small does not serve the world. There is nothing

enlightened about shrinking so that other people won't feel insecure

around you. We are all meant to shine, as children do. We were born to

make manifest the glory of God that is within us. It's not just in some of us;

it's in everyone. And as we let our own light shine, we unconsciously give

other people permission to do the same. As we are liberated from our own

fear, our presence automatically liberates others. "[2]

Now here comes the shift.

Knowing what you now know about all of the aforementioned complexities which have guided your *process* of life, I want to encourage you to **accept and recognize the value in all of the experiences you may have had** – including the painful ones. Think about some of those more prominent experiences and memories and identify how your **MESSY BeBes** shaped how you *had* perceived them.

Now choose to redefine.

You get to choose to repurpose, redefine, think differently about any experiences you had initially internalized as negative, bad, or hurtful and **choose** to see and appreciate the value in them. Trust and believe that every experience you've been allowed to have, has been a lesson and a meaningful part of *your process* that has helped mature you into who you are today and it is yet preparing you for your purpose.

Now choose forgiveness.

Forgive yourself. Forgive yourself for what you didn't know. Forgive yourself for what you may not have had. Forgive yourself for holding onto that *deepest fear* that you now realize is a lie, a lie that may have distorted your perception. And finally, forgive any and everyone else who you may felt responsible for your not being who you are created to be. They do not have that power over you, unless you relinquish it to them. Own your power and own your life.

Now be You!

You **are**, because of what **was**. Who you become from here will be because of what you intentionally change or not change (in order for it to be). You are in the *process* of being prepared for a purpose that is innate and unique to you. There is nothing you can do to stop the *process* so I encourage you to embrace it. Embrace your *process* for the good of what it has been and for the opportunities that are still yet to be. It is your *process* that will continue to create the narrative for the rest of your story. Welcome it with great expectation and choose to embrace it.

"No pain that we suffer, no trial that we experience is wasted. It ministers to our education, to the development of such qualities as patience, faith, fortitude and humility. All that we suffer and all that we endure, especially when we endure it patiently, builds up our characters, purifies our hearts, expands our souls, and makes us more tender and charitable, more worthy to be called the children of God . . . and it is through sorrow and suffering, toil and tribulation, that we gain the education that we come here to acquire and which will make us more like our Father...in heaven. "

~ Orson F. Whitney[3]

Prepared for Purpose – Embrace the Process

"Be brave enough to live the life of your dreams according to your vision and purpose instead of the expectations and opinions of others."
~ Roy T. Bennett[1]

Our journey through life is our unique, respective *process*. Everyone's *process* is a necessary aspect of their life that is designed to equip them for the next phase of their life. It is the acceptance of this process that will help begin the change to better understand and purpose the respective trials and triumphs that come along with it. That is known as experience. Randy Pausch states, "Experience is what you get when you didn't get what you wanted. And experience is often the most valuable thing you have to offer."

"Know who you are, and be it. Know what you want, and go out and get it!"
~ Carroll Bryant[2]

Once you know who you are, believe that you are the most influential person that can change your life, you have the acquired knowledge and practical understanding of how to change. If you take action toward it and mix that with faith, then change is inevitable! There is practically nothing, 'no-thing' and no one that can stop you from having a fulfilled life (lived in purpose), except you.

There is no circumventing *the process*; for everything we experience in life, though it may not seem like it at the time, is beneficial to and for us. Brian Tracy has stated and I totally agree, "Every experience in your life is being orchestrated to teach you something you need to know to move forward." Now, embrace the *process*....and proceed.

Concluding Thoughts

You are unique. You have purpose. You are here to make a difference. That is the essence of your existence which encompasses your power to impact change. Life is a series of opportunities to discover your purpose and exercise your power in the earth.

During life's journey we have been and will continue to be changed by our experiences, shaped by our truths, and stretched by our knowledge. We will be presented with choices and decisions that will continue as a constant in life. As our choices and decisions are made, they will chart the tomorrows of our *process.*

I encourage you to travel this life as a walk of faith and embrace its *process,* trusting that with every step, you are being equipped to be most successful in realizing and walking in your purpose.

Though there may appear to be real barriers and forces at work that *you could allow* to get or keep you off track, don't allow it! Help is ever present! You must choose to show up, put on your gear, and run your marathon! Continue to stride toward your goals, pace yourself as you must, but run on until you fulfill your purpose!

God Is. Therefore, no matter whom you are or what you're facing, all things are possible with Him. And it is in that which we should put our trust, hope, and faith.

Will You Share in the Process?

If you enjoyed *Prepared for a Purpose – Embrace the Process*, would you mind taking a minute to write a review on Amazon? Even a short review helps, and it would mean a lot to me.

If someone you care about is struggling, feeling stuck, or unfulfilled in their life, please send him or her a copy of this book. You can gift it to them on Amazon.

If you'd like to order multiple copies of this book for your company, school, or group of friends, please contact me at ContactUs@LeslieMHardy.com.

If you would like to invite me to speak to your group, please contact me at ContactUs@LeslieMHardy.com.

Finally, if you'd like to get free bonus materials from this book and receive updates on my future projects, you can sign up to stay informed at the book website at https://p4ap-etp.com/.

Connect with me on a weekly basis, see how I'm embracing my process and follow my schedule to join me at a live event:
Website: www.LeslieMHardy.com
Facebook @ LeslieMHardy
Twitter @ LeslieMHardy
Instagram @ Leslie.Hardy

You're being prepared for a purpose! Embrace the process being authentically you!

Notes

Chapter 1: Purpose and Process

1. https://en.wikipedia.org/wiki/Necessity_is_the_mother_of_inventi on
2. https://www.goodreads.com/author/quotes/2782.Viktor_E_Frank l
3. Viktor E. Frankl, *Man's Search for Meaning* (New York, NY: Simon & Schuster 1984), p 105.
4. https://www.brainyquote.com/quotes/cheryl_james_421502
5. https://www.goodreads.com/quotes/15990-it-is-not-enough-that-we-do-our-best-sometimes
6. https://www.youtube.com/watch?v=pj5_FCZsWGs
7. https://www.goodreads.com/quotes/2061-life-shrinks-or-expands-in-proportion-to-one-s-courage
8. https://www.goodreads.com/quotes/862088-what-we-are-waiting-for-is-not-as-important-as

Chapter 2: Elements of the Process

1. https://www.brainyquote.com/quotes/jim_rohn_133626
2. John C. Maxwell, *The 15 Invaluable Laws of Growth* (New York, NY: Hachette Book Group. 2012), p 40.

Chapter 3: MESSY BeBes

1. John C. Maxwell, *The 15 Invaluable Laws of Growth* (New York, NY: Hachette Book Group. 2012), p 39.
2. https://www.goodreads.com/quotes/46787-love-can-change-a-person-the-way-a-parent-can

3. https://www.brainyquote.com/quotes/warren_buffett_384858
4. Maxwell, *The 15 Invaluable Laws of Growth*, p 41.
5. https://www.gotquestions.org/hope-Bible.html
6. http://www.azquotes.com/quotes/topics/knowledge.html
7. https://www.goodreads.com/quotes/tag?utf8=%E2%9C%93&id=li mitations
8. https://www.goodreads.com/quotes/341532-if-you-plan-on-being-anything-less-than-you-are

Chapter 4: Choices and Change

1. https://www.quotery.com/quotes/defining-myself-as-opposed-to-being-defined-by-others-is/
2. https://www.goodreads.com/quotes/495533-whatever-you-decide-don-t-let-it-be-because-you-don-t
3. John C. Maxwell, *The 15 Invaluable Laws of Growth* (New York, NY: Hachette Book Group. 2012), p 86.
4. http://www.azquotes.com/author/21950-Nido_R_Qubein
5. https://www.goodreads.com/quotes/7733758-you-never-change-your-life-until-you-step-out-of
6. Joyce Meyer, *The Mind Connection: How the thoughts you choose affect your mod, behavior, and decisions* ((New York, NY: Hachette Book Group. 2015), p. 127.
7. https://www.quora.com/Why-do-people-fear-rejection
8. https://www.goodreads.com/quotes/496796-being-challenged-in-life-is-inevitable-being-defeated-is-optional

Chapter 5: Influences and Change

1. https://www.goodreads.com/quotes/838851-the-past-influences-everything-and-dictates-nothing
2. https://www.goodreads.com/quotes/328180-once-in-a-while-it-really-hits-people-that-they
3. Mark S. Gold, MD, "Stages of Change" *Psyche Central*, July 1, 2016, accessed June 8, 2017, https://psychcentral.com/lib/stages-of-change/
4. Todd Eliason, "Shoot for the Moon because even if you miss, you'll land among the stars" *Success*, June 28, 2009, accessed July 8, 2016, https://www.success.com/article/shoot-for-the-moon

5. https://www.goodreads.com/quotes/258199-the-purpose-of-influence-is-to-speak-up-for-those

6. https://www.goodreads.com/quotes/41544-but-until-a-person-can-say-deeply-and-honestly-i

7. https://www.goodreads.com/work/quotes/19014102-lost-lake

8. https://www.goodreads.com/quotes/7731024-you-are-not-the-victim-of-the-world-but-rather

9. https://www.goodreads.com/quotes/tag/life-quote?page=2

10. https://www.goodreads.com/quotes/tag/influence?page=5

Chapter 6: Thoughts and Beliefs - What are you thinking?

1. https://www.goodreads.com/author/quotes/7151039.Tasha_Hoggatt

2. Proverbs 4:23, NIV

3. http://www.jamesallenlibrary.com/authors/james-allen/light-of-reason/1903/july/editorial

4. https://www.goodreads.com/quotes/9821-i-did-then-what-i-knew-how-to-do-now

5. Hosea 4:6, KJV

6. https://www.goodreads.com/quotes/tag/self-limiting-beliefs

7. https://www.psychologytoday.com/basics/cognitive-behavioral-therapy

8. https://www.revolvy.com/topic/Beliefs&item_type=topic

9. https://www.goodreads.com/quotes/7924-the-reason-i-talk-to-myself-is-because-i-m-the

10. https://www.goodreads.com/quotes/468181-one-of-the-greatest-regrets-in-life-is-being-what

11. https://www.goodreads.com/quotes/search?utf8=%E2%9C%93&q=~+Kathryn+Stockett%2C+The+Help&commit=Search

12. https://www.goodreads.com/quotes/1799-the-world-as-we-have-created-it-is-a-process

Chapter 7: Power of the Mind

1. https://www.goodreads.com/work/quotes/26342027-the-mind-a-beautiful-servant-a-dangerous-master

2. Marc Van Rymenant, "95 percent of brain activity is beyond our conscious awareness", August 1, 2008, accessed May 8, 2016,

http://www.simplifyinginterfaces.com/2008/08/01/95-percent-of-brain-activity-is-beyond-our-conscious-awareness/

3. http://lonemind.com/26-experts-reveal-secrets-subconscious-mind-people-dont-know/

4. https://www.goodreads.com/quotes/7070488-the-mind-can-start-to-work-in-your-favor-or

5. Napoleon Hill, *Think and Grow Rich!*, (San Diego, California, Aventine Press, Inc.), p 213

6. https://www.goodreads.com/quotes/272578-we-become-what-we-repeatedly-do

7. https://www.statista.com/topics/979/advertising-in-the-us/

8. "Mass Media", Wikipedia, accessed September 2, 2016, https://en.wikipedia.org/wiki/Influence_of_mass_media

9. https://www.statista.com/topics/979/advertising-in-the-us/

10. https://www.statista.com/topics/979/advertising-in-the-us/

11. "Facts for Families", *American Academy of Child & Adolescent Psychiatry*, No. 54, December 2011, accessed September 8, 2016, https://www.aacap.org/aacap/Families_and_Youth/Facts_for_Families/Facts_for_Families_Pages/Children_And_Wat_54.aspx

12. https://www.goodreads.com/quotes/392307-how-would-your-life-be-different-if-you-were-conscious-about

13. https://www.brainyquote.com/quotes/brian_tracy_125750

14. "Pele", Wikipedia, accessed April10, 2016, https://en.wikipedia.org/wiki/Pel%C3%A9

15. https://www.brainyquote.com/quotes/leo_burnett_103380

16. "Social constructivism", Wikipedia, accessed April 12, 2016, https://en.wikipedia.org/wiki/Social_constructivism

17. "Cultivation theory", Wikipedia, accessed April 12, 2016, https://en.wikipedia.org/wiki/Cultivation_theory

18. https://www.brainyquote.com/authors/oliver_wendell_holmes_jr

19. Romans 12:2, NLT

Chapter 8: Change your mind, change your life

1. https://www.goodreads.com/quotes/6371-those-who-cannot-change-their-minds-cannot-change-anything

2. https://www.goodreads.com/quotes/10497-we-are-products-of-our-past-but-we-don-t-have

3. Joseph Murphy, *The Power of the Subconscious Mind*, (Princeton, New Jersey: Cambridge Publishing Group, 2010), p 19.

4. Murphy, *The Power of the Subconscious Mind*, p 9.
5. https://www.southwesternconsulting.com/roryvaden/blog/success-is-never-owned-it-is-only-rented-and-the-rent-is-due-every-day/
6. Gloria Mayfield Banks, Harvard Business School African-American Alumni Association, accessed September 10, 2016, http://hbsaaa.net/gloria-mayfield-banks-bio.php
7. http://www.azquotes.com/author/9639-John_C_Maxwell/tag/growth
8. http://www.azquotes.com/author/9639-John_C_Maxwell/tag/growth
9. https://www.goodreads.com/quotes/tag/fear?page=1
10. https://www.goodreads.com/quotes/15208-don-t-give-in-to-your-fears-if-you-do-you
11. https://www.goodreads.com/quotes/7847125-it-is-difficult-to-make-the-right-choice-if-you
12. 2 Timothy 1:7, NKJV
13. https://www.goodreads.com/quotes/29966-i-have-accepted-fear-as-part-of-life-specifically
14. https://www.goodreads.com/author/quotes/22542.Megan_Whalen_Turner
15. Kotter, John P., and Andrew P. Burtis. "Gloria Hilliard Mayfield at Mary Kay Cosmetics, Inc." Harvard Business School Case 494-016, December 1993. (Revised June 1994.)
16. http://hbsaaa.net/gloria-mayfield-banks.php

Chapter 9 : Now What?

1. https://www.psychologytoday.com/blog/here-there-and-everywhere/201210/50-quotes-perspective
2. https://www.goodreads.com/quotes/tag?utf8=%E2%9C%93&id=marianne+williamson
3. https://www.goodreads.com/quotes/search?utf8=%E2%9C%93&q=Orson+F.+Whitney&commit=Search

Prepared for a Purpose – Embrace the Process

1. https://www.goodreads.com/quotes/7954061-live-the-life-of-your-dreams-be-brave-enough-to
2. https://www.goodreads.com/quotes/479373-know-who-you-are-and-be-it-know-what-you

www.ingramcontent.com/pod-product-compliance
Lightning Source LLC
Chambersburg PA
CBHW070812100426
42742CB00012B/2335